THE TAO
OF TEACHING

THE TAO OF TEACHING

*The Special Meaning
of the Tao Te Ching
as Related to the Art
and Pleasures of Teaching*

Greta K. Nagel, PhD

DONALD I. FINE, INC.
NEW YORK

To the memory of
my mother
L. Marie Kallio

Hardcover Edition:
Library of Congress Catalogue Card Number: 94-071108
ISBN: 1-55611-416-8

Primus Paperback Edition:
ISBN: 1-55611-415-X

Manufactured in the United States of America

10   9   8   7   6   5   4   3   2   1

Designed by Irving Perkins Associates

A journey of a thousand miles begins with one step

—Lao-tzu

AN INTRODUCTION TO
THE TAO OF TEACHING

Dear Reader,

Before you read the following eighty-one chapters of this book, or perhaps after you read them, here are some pieces of background information that can help you to understand why and how this book became a book.

The precepts that you will find in this volume are based upon the messages of the eighty-one chapters of the *Tao Te Ching*, an ancient Chinese book of wisdom that is pivotal to the philosophy of Taoism. You will discover that its ideas seem familiar, for it advocates virtues (like patience, honesty, and simplicity) that have been shared by many cultures throughout the history of our world. It is, however, unique in its particular combinations of advice. Today there are over eighteen hundred interpretations of the *Tao Te Ching*, with more than sixty English translations. In addition, dozens of authors have interpreted its meaning for various aspects of living over the years. From the *Tao of Physics* to the *Tao of Pooh*, westerners have discovered how Taoist interpretations can help us better understand living in this complicated world of ours. Since Lao-tzu, the reputed author of the *Tao Te Ching*, was a great teacher, it seems to me that his work must hold important messages in particular for teachers of all kinds at all levels.

The Tao of Teaching is first of all a book of philosophy. The concepts upon which it is based, as old as they are, align well with current ideas for learner-centered practices, holistic views, interdisciplinary instruction, and constructivist education. Its precepts are important for parents, who are our children's early models and teachers, as well as for teachers and professors at all levels. Several years ago, I wrote the original manuscript for this book during my doctoral program as a way to link my course, "The Study of Teaching," with my independent studies in Taoism. My study advisor, Dr. Stephen Kim of the School of Theology at the Claremont Graduate School, encouraged me to start at the beginning, that is, with the words of the *Tao Te Ching*. In that volume the roots of Taoism are clear, unblemished by any of the intervening centuries of religious disagreements, of invented bodily practices, or mysticism. In my other class seminar, with Dr. Malcolm Douglass, we shared our respective papers with our classmates, and I was gratified by their enthusiasm about the work and its messages. "You should publish this," they said, "I can use this with my teachers," and "I can use this in my teacher preparation classes."

I chose to study Taoism as an elective because for years I was intrigued by the concept of *yin* and *yang* as related to education. As an assistant principal ten years ago, I had prepared a *yin/yang* handout for my colleagues that expressed the thought that truly good teaching was an interactive combination of evocative (leading out) and narrative (telling) practices, not just one or the other. Also at that time (1984) Art Costa explained:

> We need to transform our conception of teaching to encompass this dynamic interplay between mystical intuition and scientific analysis. So far this has not been achieved in our profession. At present, our attitude toward teaching is too *yang*—too absolute, rational, and aggressive. What is needed is more *yin*—intuition, sensuousness, and subtlety—to bring back a delicate balance. Children might then learn those other basics: the wholeness and unity of existence, the art of living in harmonious balance with nature and with each other.

The Tao of Teaching is also a book of stories, for Taoist philosophy stresses the importance of modeling, and I do want to show you, dear reader, how "real" teachers enact Taoist philosophical concepts in their daily work. The stories you are about to read are true; they are about people I have known and events that have occurred in the classrooms of three public school teachers over the years. Their names have been changed, but the anchor teachers who appear as Joe, Katherine, and Maria in the following pages are teachers who currently teach, although all three began their work in education more than twenty-five years ago. I have come to know them all quite well in recent years, but I have been acquainted with them as teachers for twenty-seven, fifteen, and five years respectively. I recognized Taoist principles in the teaching methods of Joe, Katherine, and Maria only after I thought about how I could add stories to my storyless version of *The Tao of Teaching*. I wanted to write eighty-one stories of teachers who represented the precepts of the *Tao Te Ching*, but as I began to gather incidents and individuals, I realized how choppy the whole mess could be.

One day, in the process of examining various ways to string the manuscript together, I decided that I should use individuals who represent teaching at the primary, middle, and high school levels. At that same moment I realized that I knew three people who conformed to the Tao, at least in a number of fundamental ways. Then, as their stories unfolded for me, the probability turned to certainty, and I was more than gratified—I was elated. Every day there were fascinating matches of actions and events to precepts in ways that I had never anticipated. It was almost as if each teacher had been operating with a little Taoist handbook in pocket or purse all along, although I know that was not the case. I toyed with the idea of visiting their classrooms further, making videos, and creating a publicity splash for these Great Educators—but no, in the Tao one does not seek notoriety. And in any case my experience has been that wonderful teachers who become famous stop being such wonderful teachers. So it seemed best to protect my teachers with pseudonyms rather than tell you how to look them up.

Katherine taught in three other states before settling down to teach in her current community. She has taught at Lemon School for twenty-two years, and she has run a multi-graded classroom for most of that time. Currently, she is the lead teacher of a two-room class that serves sixty-one children in kindergarten, first, second, and third grades. Here, however, students are known as "Eldests" and "Elders," "Youngers" and "Youngests" and the class is known as "ABC" because signs on the doors are left over from when the room was really two rooms, B and C, in building A. The wall between the two rooms has been removed, and the space is now part laboratory, part zoo, part library, part kitchen, part living room. In comparison, other classrooms seem hard and slick and clanky. In ABC, people are large and small, old and young, sitting in clumps and masses, high and low, on chairs and on the floor, inside things and on top of things. In ABC, the topics for discussion are often very adult—of wounded pride and piercing sadness, peace and war, anger and calm, elation and disaster—and the daily newspaper is a well-used source of information, equal in stature to the intensely personal topics shared in children's writing.

Maria teaches thirty-four sixth graders in a room that, except for a six-by-ten-inch glass in the door, has no windows. As she tells it with a twinkle in her eye, "It was a really great room when the girls with the lighted baton act performed. We can get this room *totally* dark." Room 27 is one of many "portable bungalow" classrooms at Riverview School, placed at the edge of the regular campus buildings in order to hold the increasing numbers of students, including children from local apartments, homes, and condominiums, plus thirteen busloads that arrive from barrios in two adjacent communities. Maria's students are from many socioeconomic levels and from a variety of ethnic groups. The predominant population is Latino, mostly Mexican-American, but there are many other groups of hyphenated Americans—Vietnamese-American, Cambodian-American, Laotian-American, African-American, and Euro-American. Maria has been in this classroom for only one year, but she taught for many years in both inner-city and suburban situations in two different states.

Because there is a great deal of wall space in their windowless room, she allows her students to work at desks that have been turned to face the wall and each child has a personal "bulletin board"—a large piece of butcher paper that hangs on the wall

4

above the desk, full of the students' favorite examples of current work, magazine pictures and captions, and edged with painted borders of leaves, hearts, flowers, curlicues, wavy lines, and zigzags.

Joe currently works in Room 7 at La Sierra High School. He has worked for the same school district for many years, and except for several years at another high school in a "school within a school" program, he has worked in this same room at La Sierra for his entire teaching career. Currently, he has three different preparations and five class sessions each day. This year he teaches philosophy, two sections of psychology, and two sections of government. His classroom has thirty-five desks that are typical for secondary schools in this area: wood and metal chairs, each with a wide right arm that serves as a writing surface. There is no podium, nor is there a clock. The teacher's desk is back in a corner and is used only for storage. On top of the desk are mementos from former students, a few books, as well as a couple of pictures of Joe's children.

One entire wall is full of pictures, sayings, and cartoons brought in over the years by students. Another wall contains a large photo of the earth and another huge poster dominated by Einstein's face that says, "Great minds are hampered by mediocre spirits." Next to that is a six-foot stretched-out dried snakeskin and four Ansel Adams photos. The "front" wall has a picture of a man holding a baby, an oil painting done by a 1985 graduate, a famous picture of a young Chinese man standing defiantly in front of a column of tanks during the Tienamin uprising in 1989, and a small rug from Oaxaca, Mexico, that a colleague brought Joe ten years ago. There is no particular thematic or curricular relationship among the items about the room. They are simply interesting and eye-catching.

A Bit of Historical and Philosophical Background

The story of the *Tao Te Ching* is another story that I would like to tell briefly: Almost twenty-five hundred years ago, during the

Golden Age of ancient China, a wise sage named Lao-tzu is thought to have taught in the royal courts. He was a Chinese scholar from the Court of Chou during the sixth century B.C. Many stories about Lao-tzu agree that he was fed up with the spoiled feudal princes he was supposed to inspire. They were more interested in sport and eating and drinking than in listening to words of wisdom. He rode off on a buffalo (or some say in an ox-drawn cart) into regions beyond the empire's borders. At the frontier, the pass keeper urged him to leave a record of his wisdom before he traveled on into the mountains. And so, brushing his way through five thousand Chinese characters, Lao-tzu is said to have written the original eighty-one chapters of the *Tao Te Ching* ("The Scripture of the Way and Its Virtue" and "The Book of How Things Work" are just two translations). He left behind an instruction manual for individuals to learn how to be happy and wise. Because of the book's close association to this one individual, the book is often simply called the *Lao Tzu*, although most modern scholars say that the chapters are really collections of writings and sayings by various people over time, rather than the works of any one person.

Lao-tzu and Confucius were but two of hundreds of wandering sages and wise men who instructed feudal princes and dukes. Before their time were the so-called *yin* and *yang* philosophers, whose work, based on the *I-Ching* (Book of Change), influenced the philosophies of both great teachers, who ended up being the figureheads of Taoism and Confucianism. In both, *yin* (earth) and *yang* (heaven) represent the intercourse of the fiery golden dragon and the shining silver dragon, the ancient concept of interplay of dark and light, ever-changing like cloud formations. All things carry *yin* and hold to *yang;* their blended influence brings harmony.

The Confucian and Taoist philosophies diverge on many issues beyond *yin* and *yang.* The Confucianist believes in the worldly affairs of a happy citizenry in an orderly, paternalistic system, whereas the Taoist sage believes that understanding develops from instinct and that one must respect lofty virtue, deep sincerity, a love of stillness, devotion to a worthy teacher, and wide learning. Taoism flourished in historical eras of poetry, painting, dancing, music, and it promotes those outlets in individuals.

Although Taoism is both a philosophy and a religion, the purpose of this book is not to promote Taoist religious practices. Taoism, Buddhism, and Confucianism serve as the three great Eastern philosophies. In China, people often embrace all three in their own personal philosophies. I suspect that I, too, could be more than Taoist in my own thinking. The three differ in what goals they contain for humankind as well as in their suggestions for human relationships, but all three have a concept of the Tao, or way. Nevertheless, it seems to me that in its unique suggestions for living, Taoism holds special appeal. Its philosophy is not dependent upon belief in specific gods or prophets. The Tao (the Way) in Taoism stresses virtue and wisdom; it does not seek prominence, wealth, or status. Individualism is its hallmark, but a wise individual is unassuming, simple, and artless, certainly not egotistical. One should be selfless and austere in personal furnishings. Moderation means to transcend passion, not suppress it. Immortality is won by acquiring the wisdom of acceptance, taking what comes along, for in going along with things, an individual avoids becoming separated from them.

The concepts of *yin* and *yang*, and the *yin/yang* symbol, have come to represent Taoism. All things, events, and beings are var*ying* and unequal combinations of *yin* and *yang* in unceasing motion without beginning or end.

We may see within them unity and interdependence, for *yin* and *yang* attract one another like magnets with positive and negative poles. The force of their attraction becomes greater as the distance between them becomes greater. For example, *yin* understanding and wisdom must be balanced with *yang* energy to realize their own qualities. Intuition is to be balanced with reason.

Patience is to be balanced with progressiveness. Kindness is to be balanced with the application of intelligence. There is always *yin* within *yang, yang* within *yin*. Gender is a good example of an arena where that idea is literally embodied; there are elements of *yin* and *yang* in each and every individual. Also, *yin* and *yang* are relative; something may be *yang* in one context and *yin* in another.

Taoism also encourages a deep appreciation of nature. Its poetry expresses affinity with nature and the many contrasts to be found there. Bliss is not blazing, it is tranquil. The Way emphasizes stillness, never expressing anger or greed, and the metaphor of the valley, being lower than its surroundings, represents the philosophy better than that of the mountain top. Taoism also enjoys humor, poking fun at itself and at Confucianism as well. Taoism embraces philosophies of all kinds and of every origin, yoga, folklore, art, and poetry. Conversely, its influence has been great over the centuries and it is a key to understanding many phases of Chinese life, including religion, government, art, medicine, even cooking. Taoist teachers are not well known, but that is in keeping with the humility espoused by the philosophy. The pursuit of gain and fame is not a proper human course, according to the Way.

Furthermore

Much of my personal pleasure in the Tao comes from the ways in which it helps me to reflect on various teaching practices. It not only serves as a framework for wise attitudes and behaviors, it also helps to explain why some common practices are not particularly good. Over the years, after interacting with many teachers in a wide variety of settings, I have seen some behaviors emerge as being inappropriate, even harmful, toward kids. In an era when children of more and more diverse backgrounds are our students, some practices are simply unacceptable if we want students to learn and to stay in school.

I hope to influence the attitudes of teachers who yell at their students and who fill novice teachers with advice like, "You *have* to be mean." I am anxious to stop teachers from using academic grades as rewards or punishments for social conduct, i.e., "Turning in this homework will decide whether you pass or fail." I want teachers to stop using empty threats: "The principal will suspend you if you don't stop chewing gum." I wish that more teachers realized that their putting down students is as wrong as the name-calling kids do. The coach's calling a tall ninth grader "Birdlegs" is a mean-spirited put-down. I am anxious for schools and teachers to provide pleasant environments free of odorous restrooms and old equipment. I am hopeful that teachers will take to heart the importance of their modeling. I will be grateful when teachers realize that their work is indeed social work and that students should write poetry all year long and engage in the fine arts as necessities, not "frills." I will rejoice when teachers acknowledge that children are to be treated all differently (not unequally) in spite of their similarities.

And What Else

I have enjoyed writing this book, for in the process I have discovered that I am a Taoist. Not *just* a Taoist, for I embrace ways of knowing and doing that fall under other philosophical titles, and I espouse many ideas that cut across multiple philosophies and religions, including Christianity; I am hopelessly Confucianist in my sense of social duty, and on and on, but there are indeed many traits about me and my thinking that find their source and inspiration in the Tao.

Friends call me a peacemaker. I manage to see the potential good in difficulties, and I believe that people are inherently good-hearted, so I possess quite a bit of optimism. I am quiet, or so my colleagues have said when they have worked in open-space schools with me. I am calm, or at least I seem to be calm in the face of problems. I don't like to yell and I don't much like people who yell, particularly teachers who yell at kids. I believe in the dignified equal treatment of all, and I have talked with the same courtesy and respect to school intruders in underwear or with knives on display as I have to honored guests. I also try to maintain stability and balance in my life, which often means a balancing act (I really haven't yet figured out how to move away from complexity toward simplicity). I deal with issues and people in subtle ways, and sometimes am mistaken to be a stoic Scandinavian. I try to listen more than I talk. I cultivate intuition. My life is full of interesting incidents of synchronicity, although my weekly account is not as immense as my sister's, for example, at all. I know that many things depend upon an individual's viewpoint and I believe in cultivating the ability to walk in someone else's shoes." And I believe in seeking inner peace through relaxation, as my students well know. Teachers model well and students learn well in low-anxiety environments. And some people say that I'm ethereal, while others say that I'm very practical and down-to-earth.

Ever since I was quite young my two sisters would tell me that I was like both of them rolled up into one person. Indeed, I have come to think of myself as a *yin/yang* sort of individual. My oldest sister is a forever-busy extrovert, very social, a busy mother and a teacher of learning-disabled students, an "NF" encourager who cultivates friends wherever she goes, and who is now a board member of the organization called the Friendship Force. She collects postcards, especially ones that have been sent with unusual stamps that match the picture or the message. She is fiery and golden. My other sister was the middle one, a devoted mother, a valiant fighter who died of lung cancer at the age of fifty. She was truly a book lover who read and read and read, often to the exclusion of going out. She was an introvert, an "NT" and a devoted book editor who stayed up late in her dark, book-stuffed home, working over a manuscript until morning hours with a constant cup of boiled coffee and a menthol cigarette. She collected books, turtles, and black turtleneck sweaters. She was cool, of shining silver.

I am therefore, I suppose, a *yin/yang* teacher. I am an advocate and practitioner of alternative pedagogies, yet I am confident that organized presentations of information can be successful in the context of other teaching and learning strategies. It is okay to dangle the carrot and goose them along a bit. I am a teacher-facilitator who doesn't mind doing some old-fashioned telling now and then. I have been deeply involved as a college instructor with helping students to see how learning can be done in holistic ways that involve actual doing, but I am not the least bit against telling students where the capital letters go, and why. I want my students to be free to create, to synthesize wonderful creations in their writing and presenting, but I will help them with conventions and interact with them during the creative process. I think that a caring teacher provides opportunities for rigorous projects to get done with success.

And in Closing, Before the Book Begins

The precepts that are presented in each of the eighty-one chapters are selected precepts. Lao-tzu's chapters contain multiple concepts, and are repetitious from one to the next. The idea of simplicity, for example, could be stressed in twenty chapters. In order to cull key messages and avoid being redundant, I have often left "extra" ideas by the wayside, knowing that they will be picked up in later chapters.

Someone who wants more information about how to implement the Tao might well go beyond this volume in order to find further ideas and practices. However, I have witnessed what long reading lists do to most students readers—their eyes glaze over and the list is soon forgotten within a dusty notebook on the shelf. Therefore, I would like to recommend a short list—only six books! —that could add to the influence of this work as an individual comes to understand the Tao. These titles may seem rather Western in their popular orientation, but they are entirely appropriate if you are looking for philosophical compatibility and understandable amplification for everyday contexts.

Angelou, Maya (1969). *I Know Why the Caged Bird Sings*. New York: Random House.

Carnegie, Dale (1936). *How to Win Friends and Influence People.* New York: Simon & Schuster.

Dreikurs, Rudolf (1964). *Children: The Challenge.* New York: E.P. Dutton.

Gilligan, Carol (1982). *In a Different Voice.* Cambridge, MA: Harvard University Press.

Ginott, Haim (1972). *Teacher and Child.* New York: Collier Books, Macmillan Publishing.

Hoff, Benjamin (1982). *The Tao of Pooh.* New York: Penguin Books.

If you happen to have the chance to read other books by these authors, they would be good too. I also think it is important that you not try too hard to understand the Tao. It is better that your understanding come slowly and naturally. That is why I have only included one book about the Tao, for you will be able to find many more when you wish.

In closing I have only one more thing to say, and it is through words that may be found in *The Tao of Pooh*, by Benjamin Hoff. They should help me to say why this book happens to be this kind of book and not another. Pooh has helped me to see one more way in which I might be a Western Taoist. He has been listening to the explanation that, in China, the Taoists tended to see Confucianist scholars as incomplete and unbalanced creatures who divided all kinds of abstract things into little categories, rather than reflecting the ideal of wholeness and independence. Pooh says:

"Well, let's see. The Confusionist, Desiccated Scholar is one who keeps what he learns to himself or to his own small group, writing pompous and pretentious papers that no one else can understand, rather than working for the enlightenment of others." (p. 26)

I hope you, my reader, will agree that I have not been a Confucianist in this writing.

When I hear, I forget
When I see, I remember
When I do, I understand

—ANCIENT CHINESE SAYING

1

The Way is nameless;
the name is not the Way

The wise teacher does not choose to give a particular name to her or his style of educating children. All named teaching practices have political implications, and political movements become parts of the pendulum course that education has followed throughout history. Names are limiting, for other people's definitions are attached to the names. A name can evoke unnecessary, unwarranted reactions to implied meanings that are not true of you at all. In the Tao it is important to maintain individuality. Do not follow the dictates of any one group; follow the dictates of your own, carefully developed, philosophy.

At Lemon School, Katherine's classroom is known as "ABC." The students who work in this community interact in ongoing one-on-one relationships with Katherine and her colleague Kim, and with Marlene, a longtime friend and aide, in addition to other individuals in each day's large assortment of volunteer parents. Here the dominant focus is on the individual student.

Katherine says, "I don't teach; I set up an environment in which children can grow." Children make their own choices daily, knowing that if it is morning they must do reading, writing, and math, but understanding that they *themselves* must figure out what that means. They select the activity and find the appropriate materials. They then seek the necessary help to understand techniques and enlist adult or student guidance in reaching for new concepts.

Katherine's ideas about teaching have grown from the many experiences she has had, starting with her early teaching roles in other states. She explains that over time her thinking has been influenced by the work of many individuals: Roach van Allen, Jeanette Veatch, Sylvia Ashton Warner, Virgil Howes, Malcolm Douglass, and others, including two dynamic Miller-Unruh math workshop facilitators who helped her to see learning in a new way.

She helped co-author a small volume years ago, expressing the goals of her program. The following is a brief version of her expressed ideals.

We would have all children become individuals who: possess inner-directedness with feelings of personal identity, have confidence in themselves, cherish uniqueness and differences in themselves and others, are open to experience, have highly developed communication skills, cultivate their intellectual power, use initiative and exercise imagination, are committed to constructive production of some kind, and accept responsibility for participation and action for the common good.

Adults come back to ABC year after year, former students who are now moms and dads in their thirties. They visit Katherine and tell her, "I owe my love of reading to you. I never forgot how to treat other people. I've never been bored a day in my life. Thank you so much."

In the Tao teachers and students select instructional practices and make choices that are particular to their needs, interests, and personalities, not because of the "way it's supposed to be."

One may know the insights of the Way without having to give it a name.

2

Silence is a virtue

Teachers and parents who talk too much to their children often inspire resistance that may appear in the form of "tuning out," or even as a rebellion through arguments or refusal to act. Once agreements have been made to do things a certain way, based upon shared values, teachers and students should be able to expect appropriate behaviors from one another. The wise teacher does not constantly remind the child nor does she or he criticize. Natural consequences are part of the Way.

Do not admonish harshly or lecture repeatedly. Speak once and expect to be heard.

At Riverview Elementary, Maria's sixth-grade classroom is Room 27. When it is time for lessons that involve all the students, Maria signals her students from their various places in the classroom by flipping the light switch. The room becomes very dark so the students can't help but notice the signal, and because they have discussed the expectation at their class meetings, children nudge each other to come to the gathering place on the brown carpet at the center of the room. Maria uses her quiet voice as little as possible for giving directions or scolding. She believes that she is best at simply explaining things, or encouraging kids, or saying something interesting. According to Maria, "It depends on what we're doing, but the children will learn better by seeing models or by doing things themselves."

When everyone is settled she explains, "I know you've been wondering about that big refrigerator box in the corner. It is our new classroom 'radio.' You kids who are on the decorating committee this month can make it look like a real radio, maybe one of those old-fashioned kinds if you like. It isn't working yet, though, for the schedule of programs has yet to be made. You will all have to be the producers and writers and disc jockeys and performers, and whatever. You may work alone or with one other person to think about a show that you would like to do. Some possibilities might be a talk show, maybe a local restaurant guide, maybe a show about a special kind of music. What do you think?" She pauses and waits for the hands to go up.

Good teaching can take few words.

3

Wealth breeds competition

In schools where the wealthy are in power, one often finds contests. Sometimes the contests are part of the explicit school culture: academic decathlons, spelling bees, top scores, best grades. Sometimes the contests are implicit: who wears the best clothes or has been to the best places, or who can give the best parties. In the Tao students who are compared with themselves and not with one another can be saved the dissension of competition.

Allow students to enter into the process of measuring their own growth. Honor other values over wealth to help free your children and yourself to pursue a calm life together.

Joe teaches at Room 7 at La Sierra High School. In Joe's class students fill out their own interim progress reports and often correct their own papers. No one is singled out for poor or exemplary work in his class. Joe says he doesn't want to embarrass his students or stunt them. He feels it makes students less willing to try. Joe has heard the comments when a student does get honored: "Oh, it's *him* again." The kids know anyway.

Joe always has his students assess their own work with letter grades or, for short assignments, with a check-plus, a check, or a check-minus. (Joe has come to believe that students don't work well with a grading system that involves points.) When a parent occasionally questions the ongoing student participation in evaluation, Joe doesn't back down. He confirms that this is a legitimate system of assessment—and notes that usually, if anything, the students are harder on themselves than he would be. Since the students frequently study in groups, Joe plans in the future to have groups fill out progress reports as well.

When it is time to do progress reports in the middle of each quarter, Joe does not just send unsatisfactory notes to those students who have not performed well. He changes the school form, tones it town, and gives papers to *all* of the students in order not to single out any individual. He gives comments along with grades. Finally, he has each student participate in determining his or her overall grade. Students consider their class participation in addition to three essays and two tests. Joe will initial each person's grade sheet when there is agreement, and there usually is. Joe assigns regular essays, and he believes that students learn by having a chance to correct their own papers. He tells them to feel free to write in the margins. He asks them questions like, "Is there a statement or phrase that you really like?" or, "Did you say what you meant to say? How well did you say it?" Joe takes care of assessing content. He returns to his students' essays he has graded, but he records the grade in his gradebook only; he does not put it on the paper. Each student then grades and submits the grade that seems most appropriate and Joe finds the agreement or discusses and negotiates the rare disagreements.

Freed of competition with peers, students will seek the best in themselves.

4

Application breeds learning; dig deeply

Wise teachers know that they cannot "pour it in." Children are interested learners. They enjoy finding out about new things and they are adept at memorizing certain kinds of information, as witnessed by their quick acquisition of sports statistics, lyrics to popular songs, attributes of special automobiles, or details of favorite performers' lives. When interest is high, the substance, the "stuff," is easily retained. Positive motivation is critical in promoting deep and lasting learning.

Similarly, the substance must be understood by the students in terms of its usefulness. The "stand and deliver" process of sharing substance can go only so far. It must be accompanied by the active participation of students in experiencing some aspects of the information and in gathering, using, and sharing the details.

Relate learning to your students' past or present lives, or to their perceptions of the future. Students can break into groups after "teacher-talk," and share how the new information can be applied in their lives—intellectually and personally. Always be able to answer (or, better yet, demonstrate): "Why are we doing this?"

Maria loves to experience science with her sixth graders. Although she had only two basic science courses in college, she believes it is important for kids to experience the experimentation and hands-on learning that are available through science lessons.

This fall the kids designed a nature trail that wanders around the edge of campus and identifies and explains the various plants, trees, and shrubs at their school. Maria invited a woman from the local scout council to come and work with them. The woman, whose nickname is "Roadrunner," is a local expert, and she helped Maria and the kids with the identification process as they worked with a stack of various plant guides. Each student was responsible for writing up the full description of the plant and making a pen-and-ink drawing. Then all the plants were marked with wooden stakes and numbered in order, and the descriptions were pasted, along with other directions, in the sixteen-page guide.

Maria also likes the students to do experiments that can be done in the kitchen. Plastic bags go home with her students with laminated directions and materials that might not be found in some kitchens. She has the kids report back about their "kitchen chemistry" by bringing in the results along with their written observations in their scientific journals. Safety and parental guidance are, of course, primary.

In class the kids and Maria also find ways to do research about problems that affect their lives. Air pollution comes up often, with talk of factories and cars, gases, smoke, and particulate matter. The kids decide to investigate the daytime air pollution at their school. Each child gets a plastic petri dish from a large bagful that the local college has donated to Maria's class. The students coat the insides with petroleum jelly, and they set off from school with cardboard "clipboards" and small cardboard posters that have identification numbers and explain: "Please do not touch. This dish is part of an *experiment*. Room 27." Each student sets up a study site that they choose, just so it is on the school campus and within certain areas if they are near the playground. A volunteer mom roams in one direction while Maria circulates out on the school playing field. The students record their placement data and then go inside to plan their observation schedules for the day. Everyone will "guard" his or her own project at recess times. By the third observation hour, kids are astonished at how much particulate matter has already collected on the dishes near the road at the front of the school. "Yuk!" By the end of the day all the students have something to talk and write about as they bring their dishes inside for the night. Ana summed up her thoughts in her journal: "I think we should ride bicycles instead of driving cars."

Use everyday models and encourage active participation by the students. When the Tao is applied, its depths have no end.

5

Be impartial

In the Tao, all people are "straw dogs," none more important than the others. A human failing of many teachers and parents is favoritism, showing greater approval of some children than of others. Quite often the students who remind the teachers of themselves, whether accurately or not, are the ones who receive extra attention and garner extra favors. Wise teachers are aware of the many effects of cultural backgrounds, gender differences, personality types and styles of expression.

Reach out to find points of empathy with all of your students. Encourage them all and find ways to provide equal attention with positive language and a sense of personal responsibility.

When Katherine calls students to the floor for large group times, one favorite activity is the discussion of various student writings from their individual writing books. Each child is asked permission first. Sharing of emotions permeates this activity. Katherine may read a passage from a child's work done the day before. "I had to smile about this one. Even though it's about war, I think it's a good solution." A great deal of "indirect-direct" instruction occurs in the large group seating. Chats about techniques and specific information grow out of the contexts of the children's work.

Writings are from children of all ages. The pieces of older children provide modeling, both in terms of the ideas and insights they provide as well as the greater variety of sentences. However, works of Younger and Youngest children are shared as well—and the Older and Oldest children are interested listeners. Their indulgence is perhaps out of a past easily remembered, and they do not giggle at any immature ideas or at the unusual emergent writing techniques that the younger children use.

When a first grader shared the following, everyone enjoyed the images:

> *This is a haunted house. There are seven jack-o'-lanterns and two tombstones where something died and the something is Taylor's and Brad's fish and a baby ghost likes to play there. On Halloween he floats in his cradle.*

All are creatures, some great and some small. The best is to strive from within oneself.

6

The Tao will never
wear out with use

Just as the mind does not wear out with use, the Way never becomes old or boring. Its essence is flexible and changing. Students and teachers grow in their human relationships together, through cooperative activities that reach for goals they have determined together. When interesting topics arise, the Tao allows for them to be explored, for the class is not inextricably bound to someone else's schedules or someone else's ideas about what must be taught at every moment.

Over and over again, the choices that you and your students make together in respect for one another do not get old. They get better. When planning class time, simply ask the students what should be done when.

In two of his psychology classes, Joe asks the students to help map out the curriculum for each month. He has a big butcher-paper calendar for the month on the wall. Each block is six inches square. They take class time to block out April 15 to May 15: Erikson's development, Maslow's hierarchy. They know when things are due because they write it all in large letters on the calendar.

In Joe's philosophy class the students are responsible for arranging their short reading assignments, which are kept on file for photocopying. They decide which readings to run off, and when to do them. They decide days when five are too many or three are too few. Each student keeps past readings and notes in a notebook, which then becomes a philosophy book by the end of the semester. Jay, one of the student leaders, was responsible for getting the class listed in the course catalog in the first place. He read all the material over the summer and made sure that there was a set of each reading prepared for the files. Jay is very considerate toward his fellow students. He always says, "Is this okay? Would anyone like to help me?" As time goes on, more and more students do. Not everyone steps forward right away. Several hang back, but to Joe that represents how it is in the real world.

The students bring themselves to the curriculum that is already partially structured. Joe asks, "What is this like in your own life? Imagine your family eating supper together. Draw a picture of what it was like when you were twelve years old. In some non-word way show your interactions at a meal—black arrows between individuals when they are not getting along, hearts between two who *really* get along." Joe has been asking students to involve themselves in self-expression for twenty-five years. He always stresses that there is no right way or wrong way. As he puts it, "I let comments hang out." Joe is also intent upon letting four or five other kids talk before he intervenes with a comment or question. In this way the students talk to each other, not just to him.

In the basic psychology class, students pick out topics in the text that are interesting to them. Small groups agree, narrowing the text down to five or six important chapters. He often has panels of usually three, occasionally four, kids who cover the material. If Joe feels that students have left out something that he thinks is important, he makes sure he covers it himself. Study groups meet every Thursday before a Friday test. One group meets at the local Denny's restaurant.

When he gives instructions to a group ready to present he might say, "Today we're going to present about social interaction. If something's wrong, I'll help you. The book is just a skeleton. Do something creative. I really like the class using small groups, pretending, role playing. You play the mom, or the dad, the criminal." When the time comes the students present their material in a way that is meaningful to them. Nearly every time, Joe learns something too.

It takes two to four weeks for most students to get used to the procedures. They are coming from "regular" classes in which interaction doesn't occur to this extent. What is this? It is unusual. The ones who are shy never do get to the comfort level and are afraid to speak out in discussions, but they unfold in other roles. Joe believes it is all right for some students to be listeners.

The Way is creative; its aspect changes. The spirit of the Tao is everlasting.

7

Do not think of self

In the Tao, teachers think of their students first. Their cultural diversity is an intricate challenge. Understanding their motivations helps to design the curriculum. Knowing the students, their personalities and learning styles, helps to design the instruction.

What interests you, the teacher, is not unimportant, but it cannot come first. When you show your students that you care about them, they will return your interest with interest.

Maria always asks students to sign up for five show-and-tell time slots that occur each Friday. Even though her class is a sixth grade, kids enjoy bringing things from home. The only rules: *Bring things other than toys. Make it interesting.* Some fascinating items have come from home: treasures from family journeys, grandmother's copper box, snapshots, two slide shows, a home video, coins from Mexico, ethnic food of all kinds, posters, several costumes, favorite books, several pets (many get picked up right away), souvenirs from amusement parks, sports trophies, a special fancy dress that one girl is going to wear in her cousin's *quinciñera*—her fifteenth birthday—the next Saturday.

Another activity Maria and her students enjoy over a six-week time span is the "How To," an integrated language-arts project that is based entirely on each individual student's preference of what hobby or sport or pastime is his or her own favorite, or what activity each would *like* to have as a favorite in the future. After initial research, the students interview other kids and adults who practice the activity themselves. They write a wide variety of pieces about their chosen activity, analyzing the steps and the powers and pitfalls of doing what they do. Then the kids put on demonstration speeches for each other, and eventually the class invites the whole school to the multipurpose room for the "How To" fair. All of the kids in Room 27 set up their own "booths" with various equipment as well as pages of their stories, reports, poems, and songs about their pastimes and posters that advertise the joys of doing whatever it is. Everyone is ready to answer questions, and many of the students have snapshots of themselves enjoying their activity. Visitors learn about such things as collecting teddy bears, going fishing, riding bikes, playing baseball, doing embroidery, riding roller coasters, cooking Mexican food, singing, roller-skating, collecting dolls, tying flies, riding motocross, jazz dancing, doing gymnastics, playing marbles, and more.

Maria sees students who come back after many years and who remember the time they were allowed to bring their rabbits or their bicycles to school, or the time they showed everyone else how to make enchiladas or how to skateboard.

A class is the sum of its students, not the teacher. To lead, you must learn to follow.

8

Be careful with words

The dynamics within classrooms often lead to competitive events; competition can masquerade as "cooperative" learning activities. Just as we have seen in many models of children's sports that claim to teach cooperation, the real learnings often involve victory over other children. The compliments and reprimands that teachers and parents use can produce a "sports model" for education unless care and discretion are used. The student who earns no compliment is no winner. Superlative compliments that are too general can promote feelings of ill will and competitiveness, particularly if they are worded carelessly.

In telling one child that she or he is a great student, the best speller, or the top math student, you are closing doors to other students. Instead, use words that thank children for specific acts: "You must have worked hard to put such neatness and detail in your map." "The bear pictures in your story will make the first graders happy." "Thanks for including so many figures of speech in your poem." Encouraging words are true.

In Katherine's room there are no grades on papers or report cards. The school district has supported the ABC program, noting that there is excellent communication with the systems that are in place, including a combination of the district-mandated parent conferences, the many informal conferences that happen naturally because of the well-structured parent participation program in ABC, and the ongoing portfolios that are maintained for each child annually. Notebooks of student word-processed writings and computer drawings are filed in long rows above the computers. Gigantic portfolios stand organized in king-size roll-out drawers at the northwest side of the room. Students keep records of their math assignments and writings in separate booklets that are simply sheets of appropriate writing paper stapled between sheets of construction paper. *My Personal Math Book* is just that; Katherine makes sure each student receives questions, problems, or directions for a math game that would be appropriate to his or her particular understanding at that point. Each child's writing vocabulary is entered and tracked in special books called *My Important Words*. There are many ways to evidence children's efforts and progress in ABC, but one of the most interesting and effective ways is through the public display of the children's work that changes every other week.

Children's work is *always* hanging on the walls and from the ceiling in Room ABC. During one week at the end of the first month of school, the topics that first graders are writing about include the Chicago Cubs and the California Angels, ocean animals, Ninja Turtles, a movie character called the Rocketeer, the sun, and surfing. Because Katherine insists on "steamroller writing" instead of "flyswatter writing," the children stick with one topic and provide many details about it. Every composition is accompanied by a large and colorful drawing that is almost always done first, before the writing. As many as two students may collaborate on a picture and a story, but not more than two. When the children make pictures, they demonstrate a wide variety of subject matter and techniques and they may choose to work in a large format (18″ × 12″) or an even larger format that uses paper of 18″ × 24″ or even 24″ × 36.″ The kids may use giant sheets of paper as long as they don't waste them; they will have the consequence of having to ask adults for paper if they abuse the free access to all materials that exists in ABC.

Papers on the wall are to be enjoyed. Period. There are no grades. The walls are for all kids, not just the ones with the "best" papers. There is no special section for one age group or another. The only requirement is that the papers are considered to be "done" at this point and are not "works in progress."

Communication requires dedication and patience. The Way is not to be measured. When you give your word, keep it. Like water you will bring benefit to all things.

9

The material is fleeting,
the spiritual is everlasting

The Tao recognizes that great teaching is not dependent upon fancy materials or materialistic values. A good teacher may be heard to say things like, "Give me a class of kids and a phone book and we'll do fine." The value of drawing out what already exists within the students is great. Examining the aspects of culture that go beyond the surface of dances, foods, and clothing can permit children understandings of the deeper dimensions of life.

Help your students to learn about the families, relationships, religions, symbols, stories, histories, values, and languages of various cultures, including those that are not represented in your class. Having a student's parent or grandparent share his or her life story brings deeper understanding and appreciation of the lives of others.

This year Sylvia, the student body president at Joe's school, invites her grandmother to speak in Joe's class. The grandmother was a third-generation member of her family, and she remembered when her city's Mexican-American settlement, El Campo, was a fenced-in compound. The grandma is about seventy years old, with long, flowing white hair. She has on a long dress that comes to the tops of her shoes—sandals with socks. She has on a shawl, and combs hold her hair back on each side. Her bearing is proud and she stands erect. "I can't see the ones in the back if I sit," she explains. She comments to the Hispanic kids, "You are going to be parents someday. Don't be out there gang-banging." She looks very peaceful, her dark brown face wrinkled, no makeup. She has never left the town, she says. Growing up, the boys would throw oranges at the girls. There was a Catholic church just for the Hispanics. Now it is a free clinic. Her family was a migrant family. They moved up and down the San Joaquin Valley. She started picking oranges while she was in elementary school. She married young. They had children young at age seventeen or eighteen. The area was rich with groves of oranges, avocados, walnuts. "Have you heard of César Chávez?" she asks. "He was so important to all of the farm workers." She has a big picture of him hanging in her kitchen. Before the high school was here, there were orchards and there were two streams running by. The Mexican kids had their own school, Wilton School that went from kindergarten to twelfth grade. She walks slowly around showing a picture of smudge pots in the orange groves of the nineteen-thirties or forties. The kids all tell her how much they appreciate her visit.

Like her great-grandmother, Sylvia plans on never leaving town.

Honor and integrity are not "out there"; they are within oneself. Learn to be free of unnecessary constraints.

10

Do not be authoritarian

Wise teachers have authority but do not choose to be authoritarian. They are respected by their students as fellow learners who work for the betterment of the class. They do not insist that students rely on them, but rather they help students to find ways to become self-reliant. They work together with students to find resources, share ideas, check out opinions, and do research in order to build upon experience.

Find ways for students to have power over what they learn, how they learn it, and to examine and reflect upon what they have done.

One morning ABC inherited a half-dozen bright red-and-orange-speckled amphibians. Some of the boys in the class had been playing in a park the day before where they discovered the strange-looking, three-toed creatures resting in a bog. With the help of a cautious parent, the slender-bodied animals came to school in a bucket and soon became the local attraction of the classroom, living in a plastic wading pool that another parent brought for them to live in. The search for details began: What kind of animal *is* this? Where do they usually live? What will they eat? What shouldn't they eat? What temperature is best for them? What are some safety rules that would make sense? What books can help us understand them better? Whom can we call? What kind of people study this sort of creature? How do you get a job like that? Why do they use those long names? What is a *newt?*

Eventually, pictures of the creatures and writings about them emerged. A parent talked to a biologist from the local university and reported back with more detail. Then the day came when Katherine broke the news that the newts had to be returned to their home.

Provide guidance, but do not expect students to rely on you.

11

Turn non-being into utility

In the Tao, the concept of *wu-wei* indicates that emptiness (non-being) has usefulness. Just as the space in a bowl or cup, and the vacant places of windows or doors in a building serve important functions, ideas of non-being can help teachers. The teacher who asks a question and then does nothing actually does something very useful in providing time for students to think. Silence before responses during discussions can enhance the number and quality of answers. The teacher who shares the concept of "reading between the lines," in order to see that where there is nothing there can be something, can help students learn to develop insight. To know that pauses in speaking or breaks in action can express important meanings is useful.

Provide "empty" time in a day's activities. Expect everyone to do "nothing" at times. It will provide a break from the stress of the day's activities.

Joe helped to implement the advisement program that his school currently uses so that no class time is ever used for the social and governance activities that involve kids at the high school level. Instead, every student is in a heterogeneous advisement group for twenty-two minutes a day between third and fourth periods. It is an open time used for announcements, elections such as prom court or ASB, time to honor birthdays, a brief time to relax, time for a short baseball game, time to just get to know others, to build a sense of community. One girl presented a brief piano recital. Everyone's baby pictures are on the wall. The time can also be used for counseling or going to the career center. It is free and flexible.

Each teacher serves as an advisor and stays with the same group of kids all four years. The teacher-advisor is the one who becomes knowledgeable about how the kids are really doing. There is no grade for the homeroom time except a citizenship grade. The teacher-advisors get to graduate with their kids; they wear their university colors with their graduation robes and they sit in the audience with their home group.

Joe can think of three students in his own room who would have dropped out if they didn't have someone to watch over them —to *care* for them—in this way. One student had failed English 1, and simply needed someone to untangle the way to earn credits. As teacher-advisor Joe gets a copy of all grades of his advisees to see how they are doing. Kids know that their advisor can go to a teacher or administrator when a student might not want to or be able to. When parents were surveyed, 93 percent supported the advisement program. Joe was pleased that they even knew about it. It has become rare to find parents who are well-informed about their children's lives in school, particularly at the high school level.

You must make time for "time off," and respect it. Inactivity is useful.

12

*Control input to the senses;
avoid confusion and respond to
inner depth*

We soon learn that there can be too much of a good thing. The decibels of loud music deafen. Excess in food and drink promote health problems. Working in direct sun limits the ability to concentrate.

Providing a moderate environment helps students to focus on their work and enjoy communication. Stimulating learning through various modalities is useful for some students, but these should relate to the studies at hand. Bulletin boards, music, and available learning centers can be enhancements or distractions.

Think about the relation of your environment to the students and the subject matter at hand. Provide a setting that is flexible for the students and the activities being accomplished.

Maria has set up two quiet corners in her classroom. One is in the radio corner, back behind the refrigerator carton in Room 27. Several children asked her if they could move their desks into that corner. She accepted the idea hesitantly: "Privacy helps some people, doesn't it? Let me think about this." She decided instead to try the corner out as a retreat, with room for one. One extra desk was pushed into the corner as a place for private work and thinking. People signed up by jotting their name down on Maria's sign-up sheet so she could chat with them about why privacy was important to them. The first two days with "the desk behind the box" were not pleasing. Students could sign up for an hour, but their privacy was seldom intact. Friends and not-such-friends would coast around the back of the refrigerator box in order to visit (or bother) the person at the desk. What happened over time, though, is important: after Class Meeting conversations exposed the interlopers, the "visitations" gradually stopped. The radio corner truly became a private place after another week.

The other private corner is behind Maria's desk, by the door. She talks about how, after she read about the calming effects of pink walls on violent offenders in public institutional containment facilities, it occurred to her that it would be a good idea to think about the effect of colors in her classroom. Even though Maria doesn't love pink (she is a peach and green fan), she decided to create a peaceful pink area by her own desk for her children who would either enjoy or require it. The best result, she now realizes, is that it is also *her* corner of the room, and she knows how important it is for the teacher to be calm. She makes a point of spending at least one daily segment of time in her relaxing atmosphere. Some days she comes to school early; some days she purposely stays away from the teachers' common room at recess; other days, she eats her sack lunch in the classroom; on Fridays she spends time after school just thinking about the week that has passed and the week to come.

Use your senses to look inward.

13

Love others as you love yourself;
accept uncertainty

Showing others the same concern you would desire for yourself is a concept that is common to all of the world's great religions.

Showing students that they are loved is a gift that wise teachers may give their students. Love does not have to be demonstrated as syrupy affection, nor does a teacher need to become a parent. Rather, the Tao provides enjoyment in reflection, caring, and respect. Developing self-love is also critical for teachers. Victims of low self-esteem may find it hard to reach out to others.

The wise teacher also knows that days with active students seldom turn out exactly as planned. Forces of individual personalities, interruptions and plans that are imposed from outside the classroom, and variations in your own feelings about how things should go make a difference in what really happens.

Respect your own individuality and be proud of your work as an educator. Consider your students, and know that change will always be part of your regular routine.

Katherine can seldom be found in her classroom, even though she is physically there from six o'clock in the morning to five in the afternoon most days. The reason she can't be found is that, except for large-group carpet times, she is always out among the children, moving about from one spot on the floor to another as she coaches them about their work. She believes that the students will achieve and understand more from receiving personalized assistance than from large-group direct instruction. Katherine has an internal sense of where students can go next in their studies. Combined with her experience in knowing what motivates the kids, her intuition helps Katherine jot down appropriate learning tasks/ questions for each child. Some of the inquiries are even co-designed, because many students have a sense of what data they would like to gather in their classroom. A child may only have one or two questions to answer in a day, but because of their complexity as problems, requiring careful data collection and thinking, each may take an hour for the child to accomplish.

Because of the many specialized creative tasks that Katherine performs, it is naturally very difficult for substitute teachers to fill in for her. Fortunately, she is seldom absent.

14

The Way is subtle;
respect and apply the past

Respect the past in order to understand the present. The two cannot be separated.

As teachers learn about the personal and cultural pasts of their children they can interweave their knowledge into the choices for curriculum and the designs of lessons. Continuity with a child's past will make school seem a natural, accepting place. The child whose home was full of mother's "schoollike" talk and explanations will find it much easier to adapt to hearing more of the same at school. The child whose pre-school experiences were full of caretaking and affection, but little cognitive "patter," will benefit from lessons that relate somehow to things that are more familiar —foods, stories, television shows, relatives, advertising. Wise teachers respect the past in their other decisions as well. What is "old" is not necessarily outdated.

Try to refer to the past experiences of your children in order to make the transition from home to school a comfortable process. Reflect upon practices and materials of the near and distant past to enrich your thinking about what is appropriate to do in the present.

Joe asks students to share important moments, events, or discoveries of just the past week and he enjoys watching the entire class connect with similar or related stories. They are quickly hooked. Sharing the students' lives is automatically interesting and motivating. He'll ask questions like, "What happened to you that made a difference? How did your week go? What made it good? What do you wish you hadn't done?" Not everything gets said out loud. Often he has the kids write: What was a special moment that happened in any other class? Was there any moment in your life that you would relive if you could? What would it be? Does one of you want to share?

One boy remembers he was put in to play shortstop late in a Little League baseball game. He had never played shortstop before, and with the bases loaded a screaming line drive came his way. He dove for it—and he got it. His team would have lost if he hadn't. One girl shares how her grandmother took her shopping for the first time in East L.A., and she wanted to relive that moment. A boy, an immigrant from the Middle East, says that his mother died eleven years ago when he was only seven years old. No one in the class even knew that he didn't have a mom. He is the sort of person who seldom talks. He says he has never felt right about not taking her funeral seriously; he had acted silly and actually laughed at her burial. His father is from Jordan and there was no talking about it. A classmate suggests, "Why don't you go see her?" So he does. He goes to see her grave and it helps him say the things he could finally put into words.

In Joe's Psychology A class, every single student gets to tell his or her life story. Each individual takes one full class period. Students are responsible for researching the information and making it clear and interesting. Most everyone would rather have two days, but Joe thinks that a total of five weeks to get through the entire class is about right. This is one of the classes where the students help with the scheduling on a huge calendar on the wall and their names get filled in for their slots early in the semester. Joe is always amazed at how much information comes out of the students' experiences. There are constant teaching moments. They all talk about school, family, mobility, the effects of major events, family dynamics, communication, high school experiences, often referring back to each other's stories: "We had that in my family, too." They can remember which student has how many brothers or sisters, who has done well in school, who has had trouble. Joe weaves in the academic concepts. Once all the students have told their stories, they are assigned a major paper about "what we all have in common," and they discuss it. When it is finished, and the students have come to know each other, Joe asks, "How can we afford *not* to tell stories?"

Stories are not limited to psychology classes. Students in Government will participate in their own version after the Advanced Placement test.

One girl, whose mother was killed in a robbery a few years before, did more teaching than Joe could have done with the topics of anger, loss and mourning, crime and punishment. In telling the story the girl relived some of her emotions from that terrible event. In the end, however, she has forgiven the murderers, a man and a woman, who are now in jail for life. Joe, incidentally, knows one of them; she was in his Government class several years ago.

For the students, the past and the present are inseparable. Look to the past, sometimes distant, for present understanding.

15

*Be cautious, reserved, flexible,
sincere, honest*

Wise teachers think before acting and speaking toward students, modeling ways that demonstrate the same courtesy extended to adults. They are calm about personal issues and relations, but excited about things that are being discovered and learned. Wise teachers can change with the needs of the context, realizing that certain ways of teaching do not fit all students, and some kinds of consequences are inappropriate for entire groups. Being "real" with students is important, for they are able to sense the phony and they resent inauthentic comments.

Do not lie to students or their parents through shaded recollections of events, empty threats, false promises, or insincere compliments.

Maria believes that the art of her teaching comes from being raised in a family of teachers, although she has several good friends who believe that they were "born" teachers through being the eldest in a sibling group, or that several life experiences (like tutoring, playground work, church projects) have shown them that they are "naturals." The ability to act honestly with children is fundamental to her.

She figures that most of her science teaching comes from several key experiences in her education. She is particularly grateful for getting to work with several funded summertime projects over the years, in writing and literature, science and math. It was the science project that included opportunities to make and view videos of herself in a process of interaction analysis. She had to analyze her behaviors with kids as well as the words that went along.

Through both avenues she has come to see how important many teacher behaviors are. She never yells across the room to scold a child nor does she threaten her students with punishments like suspension. Suspension, if it does have to occur, is for serious offenses and she has come to question it as an effective consequence. On the other hand, she sees how important her positive acceptance of students and their answers are. She has learned about the dangers of complimenting kids in front of one another, for to honor one child is to exclude the other, difficult in any family or community. Because she has never forgotten the importance of positive support, Maria does take the time to be complimentary, but instead of saying much in class, she chooses to make "good" phone calls to children's homes on a regular basis. Early Friday evening usually works for finding families at home. She has never found her calls to be anything but warmly received. When Maria "threatens" to make a phone call home, it is a good sign, not a bad one.

Be wary but yielding. Express yourself naturally, and accentuate the positive.

16

Know one's own roots to embrace others

In working with students who have wide varieties of cultures or roots, wise teachers learn about their own roots and share their reflections. Teachers who do not know how varied and strong their own values are cannot realize the impact of their values in judging others. Personal past heritage and present perspectives always affect what teachers teach, when and how they do things, and what they care about.

Take the time to explore your own heritage and write or tape your own autobiography. Share with other teachers as well as with your students.

The calendar on the wall showed that Joe would be the one to tell his story on April 20. It also just happened to be his birthday. Presto! Joe got his day. So he scrounged a carousel slide projector and sat with boxes of old slides for two nights. He brought his own "This Is My Life" show to school: a slide show of his life on his fifty-first birthday. At age thirteen he's holding a fish. (Before Joe was thirteen there was no family camera.) Then all the camping trips, high school graduation pictures. "Where is that? Did you like it? What was the weather like? What did you eat? What were you driving? How long did you stay? Which was your favorite sport? Which would you like to go back to?" Joe told his parents' story. His brother's. His sisters'. "What are they doing now?" His high school homecoming parade with five cars. St. Joseph's Academy, 1961. Ten guys were in his class, that's all. All dressed exactly the same in blue Levis, cuffs rolled up, plain white T-shirts. One is now the chief of police and one is now the mayor. The entire senior class had ten guys and nine girls in this tiny little school in Prescott, Arizona. The army. A number of slides from Vietnam. Vietnam was quite powerful for the students—the people, the water buffalo, the streams, the villages, a lot of scenery. The kids got very quiet. "Vietnam for them is like World War Two for me," says Joe. "Here's my car, an Impala station wagon. Eileen and I got married. Here we are, camping in the Rockies. Here's a guy fifty years old. Here's my dog. Here's thirty-five years of my life." The show took him hours to prepare and he is really glad he did it.

At other times during school Joe is not afraid to allow kids to ask him rather personal questions. They don't come up often, but when they do he deals with them: "Have you ever cheated?" They just want a yes or no. "It never comes up in a vacuum," Joe says. "We're talking about cheating or drugs or other opinions." In time he probes the students: "Hasn't everyone lied about something? We are human." The relationships he develops are very deep.

Find ways to understand your basic nature.

17

Have faith in others so they
will have faith in you

Faith does not survive where there is criticism, suspicion, or fear. The wise teacher treats all students as if they were deserving of respect. Their treatment of their teacher can be respectful and gratifying in return. The teacher-student relationship in the Tao promotes doing activities together as opposed to having the teacher play the role of primary giver and doer.

Have faith in your students' responsibility for learning. It will allow them to fulfill your expectations.

Katherine believes that children learn many things through their own creativity and play. Among the many activities that allow children to assume responsibility in ABC are the blockhouse and lunchtime drama times.

Choosing to be in the blockhouse is an opportunity that may arise once or twice a month for any child. Three students may sign up together on the sign-up sheet in order to spend a full morning in this corner of the room, building with the one-foot to three-foot-long wooden blocks, designing situations and playing them out, and then inviting visitors in to tour the premises. Talking, planning, and imagining together, the children create and re-create new environments. They enjoy what they are doing and, as two Oldests explain to me, it is also fun "not to have to do regular work that morning."

Choosing members for lunch-hour plays is another possible way for children to express themselves. During every lunch hour children have the opportunity to come back into the classroom from the playground in order to create and practice skits and plays. The play is usually thought up, continually ad-libbed, and produced in one week, with a final production acted out before the rest of the class on Friday. Christy, a Younger, gets to be the mom in her play about the mother with three children. The good sister and the bad sister are both Youngests and the active baby is the only member of the group who is an Older.

On Friday afternoons time is allotted for the week's new productions. One mother comes on Thursdays to advise the different groups that choose to do dramas, and although she encourages them to employ various conventions, the children have a strong voice as to what they will do and who is going to do it. Most of these self-selected dramas portray the trials and tribulations—and foibles—of real life. They are often in the vein of "I Love Lucy," "The Carol Burnett Show," and "Father Knows Best," and the plots center on everyday life. The characters in the various plays are mostly girls, although boys do come now and then, or they are enlisted to join in for specialized roles. For some reason, tales of animals, kings, and imaginary beings seldom emerge.

Believe in one another.

18

*When the Way is not followed
or family relationships are not in
harmony, hypocrisy and pious
advocates arise*

The Tao is not decided by forces outside the classrooms of wise teachers. However, when harmony is lost—when the close social climate of a classroom is not achieved—outsiders will use the opportunity to propose practices and activities that would be inappropriate and deleterious to the Tao. The voices of many "experts" and high-level committees from government and business insist that our country's educational progress is not competitive with other industrial nations, that standardized test scores are the best measure of achievement and they are not high enough, and that excellence can be found only within a canon of certain studies.

Provide a truly excellent education for your students, in spite of the "excellence" advocates.

Katherine has always had her students' parents participate in the daily program of ABC. With her devoted learner-centered approach, it is necessary to provide assistance through the helping hands of parent volunteers. Because children come from many different neighborhoods in the city, as well as from other towns on interdistrict transfers, parents are from many diverse groups. And although children's ideas and choices guide much of the regular curriculum, the ever-present parents influence learnings in ABC as well. Parents are always welcome to sit on the "hot seat" at the front of the room—the same small student chair that Katherine uses for large-group times. Anyone in the classroom is encouraged to ask the individual in the hot seat a good question. Parents also give formal presentations, read books, or even put on shows. Parents are also responsible for designing special projects, especially crafts, art, drama, dance, that children may sign up to do. The information and understanding that they bring to the children are varied, rich, and deep.

At least three times a day, the large open space at the center of the double room becomes a meeting place for all. Katherine calls everyone together with the same approximate signal each time. She plays middle C, E, and G on the piano, striking each note with force, pausing in between notes to permit each sound to die away before the next note is played. Then she hits the chord. Students encourage each other to leave their books and papers and settle on the floor, sitting wherever they choose in clumps and rows that face the plain wood and metal student chair where Katherine always sits. Katherine seldom stands before the group. The day's parent volunteers who have been working in this area, propped against their backrests like so many grownups on the beach, usually remain just where they are, and the children who have been working near them usually stay nearby. Their own sons and daughters sit close, Youngers and Youngests often sitting in laps of their moms or dads. Adults who have been working in other sections of the room pull up small wooden chairs to sit at the rear edges of the area.

One day Sean's mom came to school with him and they got up in the front at large-group time. Sean held a large shallow basket with a hooped handle that was difficult for him, a slight Youngest boy, to manage. He was, however, proud and determined. Then his mother and he began to tell the story of how his family celebrates his "Airplane Day." Five years earlier, this very day was the day that his plane arrived in Los Angeles from Calcutta, India, carrying him at the age of five months, along with one other baby boy of the same age. The two infants, who had come from an orphanage and had flown all the way with a supervising nun, had nestled in the basket that fit an airline seat perfectly. For two days the two basket occupants traveled, wrapped tightly in blankets. Sean's mom described the nervousness and joy that she and her husband experienced at the airport as new parents. With her son's help, she also told about India, the country of his birth. The children asked many questions and satisfied their curiosity about India and about orphanages. They also learned about the excitement of a woman over forty getting to choose a child she and her husband really wanted.

The kinds of things that children and parents choose to do in ABC are always creative. There are no dittos in this classroom. Everything is created, whether by a student or one of the many adults who populate the room. Moms or dads are often either on the hot seat or they arrange for guests or special events. Their enthusiasm often impacts the large-group time in ABC. A mom who loves to do storytelling comes to share regularly, and one father who is also a storyteller volunteers his services several times a year. A mom and a dad put on a puppet show for the class in honor of their daughter's birthday. Other people tell about their occupations, and one dad gave a most memorable lesson when he shared with the children a detailed description of the kinds of people he tries to help in law enforcement. A Japanese-American mom shared a fascinating children's storybook from her country. The writing was in Japanese, but she translated into English and pointed out how its illustrations carried the message. Parents are present in ABC every day of the week, mostly in the morning, but they are welcome all day.

Seek information from the source. Didacticism is not a substitute.

19

*Reduce selfishness, have few
desires*

The wise teacher doesn't hire an orchestra when a guitar will do. Expending effort in a multitude of arenas means that energy and time can be lost to the development of the Tao. Sometimes teachers work extra jobs or devote hours to their homes or social lives, much to the detriment of reflecting upon their classes with a quality and quantity of time. Wise teachers select natural pastimes that will complement interests and projects related to teaching. The Tao includes many possibilities, from the teacher who enjoys sharing reading with students or who loves to explore seashores and mountains for shells and stones, to the one who travels to learn about the similarities and differences of various climates and cultures.

Find pastimes that can enhance your personal satisfaction with teaching. Don't use the false concept of "time off" during holidays to drain your financial and physical resources into pursuits that draw you away.

Maria worried about how her teaching career would change after she and her husband had children of their own. She knew that the first ten childless years of her marriage enabled her to do many things with, and for, her students. Her many field trips with students to museums and city landmarks after school, and her different outreaches to neighborhood meetings at nights and on weekends, to school carnivals and festivals, to roller-skating parties, or to students' homes, would be more difficult to take when she was a parent. Nevertheless, the ways in which Maria remained open to her students helped her to see that her school obligations could help, not hurt, her home relationships.

Maria's husband agreed to go on some of the trips that became more like family outings than school field trips. A Friday evening visit to a children's repertory play in a nearby town, and then to the home of one of the families, meant that their whole family went as part of a larger carpool group. Bringing her baby to most school events was not only possible, but it became an anticipated pleasure for students in Room 27, a chance to meet the teacher's new baby.

Maria has five favorite kinds of places: gardens, mountains, beaches, museums, and libraries. She feels very fortunate to live in a community that allows her access to all, and she never has to spend much money in order to pay a visit. She always comes away with peace of mind and something she can share with her students. Even though she has traveled in foreign countries, her fondest pastimes can all take place close to home.

Simply walking out the door renews her spirit and allows her mind to leave any troubles for the while. It is a pleasure noticing the new blossoms on the rosebushes, finding a stone path that the children have constructed, watching a blue jay on the fence, standing by a peach tree in the dried grass, a simple breeze cooling her cheek. She enjoys sharing the fruits of her garden as well. She brings apples to her students in the fall. Not many of them ever knew about the star in the center until they cut them open in Room 27 during their week of "Apple Days" when almost all of their studies had something to do with apples. Pomegranates are for eating outside, everyone covered by an old towel they had brought from home. What did the ancient Greeks think about them? Oranges are for eating and for starting a unit on printmaking. What happened to all of the orange groves? Loquats are usually a surprise to everyone. They taste good and their large, dark, smooth seeds are somehow appealing, simply beautiful to everyone. They even make good glossy stones for playing African *mankala* games later.

Manifest plainness, embrace simplicity. These are the ways to seek wealth in experience.

20

Do not see things in black and white

The context and the culture make a difference. Seeking to understand circumstances can be illuminating. Behaviors and values that appear clear-cut in one setting may lose their importance in another. One child's profanity may be another child's daily affectionate slang, one teacher's prohibition may be another teacher's pleasure, one parent's rudeness may be expected assertion to another. A classroom full of learners can make its own rules about both schoolwork and behavior. In this way rules can be changed as the needs of the group change.

Learn to withhold judgment and see actions and events only as part of a larger context.

Joe believes in having different rules for different kids—aside from the official school rules, that is. In some classes it is okay for work to be late. Sometimes he will postpone a test if the students ask ahead. For example, his Advanced Placement students had a big term paper due in another class, so he changed the due date for his test to the following Monday. According to him, it is okay to ask what other teachers are expecting from the kids. It is a matter of respecting the students.

"Would anyone like to help make the rules? Go to someone else's house tonight." He is glad that kids are allowed to talk in certain sections of the library, because then he can send them to do group work. Good rules are not invariable, for if they are truly fair, they are sensitive. For Joe, that is part of learning, especially for what he teaches. What is the difference between a rule and a law? In daily homeroom, questions are asked: What are the rules? Are they fair? How do we change rules that aren't? Joe also knows that the arrangement of desks has a lot to do with what goes on. He has five different seating arrangements for five different classes. First period, circle. Second, modified square. Third, similar. In his AP class, lecture rows limited to three facing front. Fifth, circle. Joe's rule is that if there is an empty desk in front of you, sit in it.

Joe has never sent a kid to the office. He has never sent anyone to detention, and never to "Saturday School." Eating or drinking in class? They are okay because Joe himself drinks coffee or a Coke sometimes. He believes standards should be shared. Just clean up after yourself. He has separate containers to discard glass, paper, and cans.

Rules go on all the time, though. The Golden Rule. Joe does have other standards that he expects without variance: Nobody writes unless we're all writing. Nobody reads unless we're all reading. Don't do your homework for another class. No sleeping. There must be engagement, community, understanding. When a conversation gets heated, for example, when the topic is abortion and everyone, even the very quiet students, has something to say, Joe watches the clock and begins a process he likes to call "Quote Without Comment." Everyone in the room says one thing without rebuttal. Joe knows that the process just lets the air out of an inflated balloon that would otherwise explode.

He likes to emphasize an idea from Rousseau: Authority comes from the community, not the individual; but individuals of integrity must support the community.

21

The Way is real, but elusive;
intuition leads

The Tao does not always deal with measurable, observable phenomena. The best thing for a child to do in a given day may not be the next linear event in an externally predetermined sequence. Just as scientists do not get their ideas and achieve their findings through the structured perfection of the steps in the scientific method, students do not gain understandings through clear-cut connections. Knowledge is gained in much more personal ways: 1) through the cognitive connections that join new knowledge to prior knowledge in the shifting organizations of the mind, and 2) through hunches that lead to thoughts that seem appropriate and may be supported in retrospect by empirical information.

Learn to trust your own feelings and encourage activities, such as brainstorming, that allow personal insights to be respected in your class. Encourage your students to keep journals that trace and reflect these developments.

Maria is convinced that if her students write in journals they will have a healthy outlet for thoughts and feelings, and they will not need to find other overt and bothersome ways to deal with some situations. Her class agreed upon twelve full minutes of free writing each day, and although she does not assign a topic, she asks volunteers if they would like to tell what they're planning to write about that day. She knows that some students appreciate the idea, not so much because that's what they end up writing, but it gets them thinking. The students know that their journals are not graded for content or correctness, but each day is for writing at least a page. If the new entry doesn't fill the page, the rest of the page may be used to explain why it was difficult to fill a page that day.

Several days a week she encourages journal sharing, sometimes just with a partner, sometimes with a small group or the whole class, always an individual choice, always voluntary. She also makes overhead transparencies of anonymous entries in order to have children see, and not just hear, others' entries. The various entries are not always the best models, but she never puts up work that would be an embarrassment to any student in her widely heterogeneous class. When a simple piece of writing has a good attribute to highlight, Maria uses it. And sometimes the writing that comes from a casual journal session for her sixth graders is greatly entertaining. Maria picked a poem out of William's journal to share with everyone:

> *I clutched the remote in my palm*
> *Then pressed a button and turned it on.*
> *The dark room became bright*
> *The walls moved with changing light.*
> *I gazed upon the sacred screen*
> *Lucille Ball and James Dean.*
> *I slouched back in the sofa bed*
> *And placed a pillow to rest my head.*
> *The perfect place; a reality diversion*
> *Right in front of my television.*

The Way is mysterious and elusive, but its essence can reveal high moral cultivation.

22

Teach by example

The power of modeling has been demonstrated over and over again in various educational settings. Its impact in applied situations is vivid: children who select a book at the library because their teacher read it enthusiastically the week before; teens who really do "say no" because of refusal patterns learned in drug resistance programs; adults who practice techniques of water, plant, and animal preservation because of their week in the mountains at elementary outdoor education. The parent or classroom teacher who is intent upon showing rather than just telling will enhance academic recall and deepen understandings of real life.

Maria knows that her modeling during silent reading can be powerful. She is a real participant when her kids have their daily Sustained Silent Reading, or SSR time. At first it made her nervous to be enjoying a book during class time. It didn't meet her "Puritan" standards for herself as a hardworking teacher. But after doing the reading for a full week, sitting in different places around the classroom rather than just at her desk while she read, she came to see the many advantages it held for her students and for herself. The kids are always curious about the books she reads, and although some weeks she reads one or two picture books a day, other weeks she tries to keep up with her love of biography or historical fiction. When she read *The Autobiography of Malcolm X*, as told to Alex Haley, kids asked questions for days. The movie was available, and although most of the kids hadn't seen it, they had heard all sorts of stories and wanted to know more about. Her reading always managed to enliven another lesson during the day in some way: a beautiful picture to share, a funny incident, an interesting quote. The children know that Maria is a lover of reading. She treasures her time with books each day, and the other things she might get done during these quiet moments can be done, sometimes more efficiently, with student help at another time of the day.

Practice what you preach; thereby you may become whole with the environment.

23

Use few words

The Tao encourages the teacher to use evocative words and subtle questions, calling forth the ideas, the problem-solving ability, and the dedicated work of the students. The teacher who encourages students to participate and who practices the art of listening will be successful. Teachers certainly have words that are important for their students to hear, but they must choose them carefully and use them sparingly—to attract students to ideas, to encourage them to go on, to point them in positive directions. In a discussion, the teacher may allow two, three, or more students to speak or respond before he or she speaks again. Students will feel important and credible.

Think before you speak; ration your own words. Remember, you are one of many.

Now and then, Joe imposes a rule on his own behavior. He allows himself only three comments during an entire class period of fifty-five minutes. What he has found is that the students do better, particularly when they are in circumstances that permit heated interchange. Topics that can engage all students at all ability levels are the way to start, such as, "Should we even have a homecoming queen?" The point is that the teacher should not be responding all the time, and even then the teacher should use words sparingly. Then the conceptual difficulty can gradually build to issues, for example, on a national or international scale.

Joe has a sophomore student named Casey who is knowledgeable and insightful. For a while he seemed pompous and egotistical. He talks about pulsars and quarks and other similar concepts in the context of other ideas. Mathematically Casey is a wizard. When he gets going, everyone has to get out of his way. His style is to make bold, broad, political remarks. Sometimes the other kids get upset. When the kids were talking about tension and emotions, Casey said, "Did you know that trees grow up because gravity pulls down?" Some kids warm up and roll their eyes, others get upset. Joe keeps things together. It doesn't bother Joe that Casey sits on top of his desk. Casey isn't very tall, so he doesn't block visibility for other kids.

From the same class, a senior named James decided to drop out of school. James told Joe that he would be leaving school before the end of April. He's taking the proficiency test; he doesn't want to go through graduation. He doesn't care about the Grad Night party. He is going to Minnesota for a month to live with an aunt and uncle and then he's going to take off and just *wander*. The parents both live at home, but they are not interfering. They don't like James's plan, but they won't stop it.

What James thinks he'll do is go stay at a couple of communal farms in Texas or Kansas. There, everyone earns his or her keep. The kids say, "Wow, you're kidding." But Joe noticed that Casey had a tear trickling down his face. Joe waited for ten minutes, then Casey said that he felt like a little boy, he was in such awe of what James had said. These moments of beauty don't escape Joe because he spends as much effort in watching and listening— body language, facial expressions, where the students' eyes are looking, how they're breathing, or what their hands are doing. But the most important moments are usually spent in silence.

Most teenagers don't see themselves as very important. They feel good if they are appreciated. If Joe had been talking or carrying on, he would have missed the story and the scene. Before the class ended, James said, "Casey, why don't you go with me?" At the end of class, students leave slowly. They walk up to students who have said something special and acknowledge it privately, quietly give a hug or a pat on the back. Guys shake hands with those who have said something that touches them. Joe erases the board, takes a deep breath or two, and gets ready for the next class.

James also takes Philosophy with Joe. The next day, James told the class that Friday would be his last day. The class put on an impromptu graduation ceremony. At eight o'clock on a misty gray Friday morning James came in. The students put him on Joe's swivel chair in the middle of the room. He had a ski beanie on his head that a girl had given him, covered with yellow wildflowers sticking out of it. One guy stood up on his desk and read two poems from *The Road Less Traveled*. Another boy who had been in fourth grade with him gave him a picture. Each person said one thing to him. One girl gave him a flower. Then he asked if he could say one thing to each person. One at a time, he gave everyone a hug. Everyone joined hands and danced to the music of Joe's outback tape. Joe has outback instrumental music that his sister Mary played at her third wedding.

Tired. they sat on the floor. Many of them, especially the young men, were crying, for he had been mostly a friend to the other boys. The more powerful embraces had come from the boys. The bell rang and second period came right in. That was it. A self-contained, spontaneous ceremony, never to be duplicated. Ever.

Later another teacher said, "I heard what happened in your class. God, I've never seen James's face that radiant!"

Keep your eyes and ears open. It is nature's way to say little.

24

Progress is slow; do not boast

Human growth and learning is either of an evolutionary nature or it consists of revolutionary leaps that occur rarely. The teacher who frequently spends a great deal of time testing student progress is using valuable time that might better be spent in learning activities. In an environment that promotes learning, assessment is ongoing and occurs concurrently with learning activities, rather than only at the end of "units of study." Individual students move at varying rates and they achieve concepts in personal orders. Similarly, the wise teacher does not engage in self-promotion, for it is the sign of an insecure person.

Encourage students and do not claim their successes as your own.

Joe thinks that there are some important questions to ask about classrooms: Is there student success beyond teacher evaluation? Whose things are on the wall? Who speaks for the class?

When Joe talks about class interaction, he mentions the metaphor of a pinball game. Class is a pinball game and Joe pulls the plunger for the first kick. In pinball the first kick doesn't win the points. Joe is the catalyst, unless a student happens to come in to class with the first question or issue. Students have permission to do that. The kids are the flippers.

Bing bing bing bing bing bing. All of a sudden someone has said something that . . . Erikson . . . bing bing bing bing . . . Maslow . . . taught the guy . . . who makes absolute sense . . . bing bing bing Joe always calls on them. And they almost always speak.

For Joe, evaluation is ongoing. As he works with kids, intuition builds. Everything is part of assessment—as long as it is not something private—and can include a smile, a facial expression, calling on someone else. Joe knows that something registers in his head, patterns form. He just comes to know. Joe remembers things over the ninety days that each class meets, and students never question their grades with Joe. The students know too.

At the end of the semester Joe does spend a relatively short time assigning grades to his 175 students. Even then, kids dialogue with each other about grades and about the grading policy. They spend about an hour of class time talking about grades in community. "Who gets the highest grade when there are people working together? Someone who keeps the community intact? Someone who makes suggestions for activities and keeps discussions rolling? Someone who has a sense of what is going on, who reads on their own, who shares, who . . . ?"

"In Philosophy, this guy Jay gets upset if we don't read every day. He serves as a guardian in many ways." Joe is constantly reflecting, and he thinks in terms of letter grades, not congregates of points. Actually, students take care of their classes in many ways, including assuming responsibility for sharing timely newspaper articles. Although she doesn't care for short-notice jobs, the woman in the photocopy room will nevertheless run things for Joe's class if a student brings in an article needed that morning. "My favorites, if I have any," says Joe, "are the students who read the newspaper before they come to class. It's amazing what can be taught out of the daily paper."

Over the years, in retrospect, this style of teaching has prepared them really well, students say when they come back to Joe's school. Nevertheless, there has been no measurable difference on standardized test scores. The kinds of things that Joe expects have other carryovers, however.

For AP class, on the other hand, the work is tightly structured for the test that follows: read a chapter over the weekend, outline, study guide, three essays a week, Friday is test day. It is a self-study program in some ways. The kids volunteer their homes and the parents provide treats as the kids study Thursday nights. Joe is home reading essays on Thursday nights while the kids are in study groups. Together, they review for the AP test itself for over a week. All but one of Joe's students is taking the test and that is a vote of confidence in the program. If the kids were not feeling good about spending seventy-one dollars of their own money, they would not sign up. That is a form of evaluation in itself, and the students do well on the actual test; the pass rate is high each year.

Joe begins every AP class session asking someone a question. The atmosphere of the room is typical "Joe's room," but the arrangement is slightly different. The desks are arranged in three rows. "Never have more than three kids deep. I don't like them looking over people. They can't hide, they can't sleep, no desks are placed against the wall." Joe wants people leaning forward, thinking forward. There is no one in a back row. Joe doesn't show movies; he will recommend some for them to watch at home, and instead he will go to the chalkboard. He does, on occasion—perhaps three or four times a semester—play educational videos like *Remember My-Lai*, a tape on why men in groups will do what they won't do as individuals. Bill Moyers on Robert Bly, a guru of the men's movement. Joe wants to set up opportunities for the kids to react. He plays tapes of Beethoven's Ninth because he feels like it. Last week he played the music to the movie *Dances with Wolves* because he loves it, and it's easy to write to. Music helps on test and essay-writing days.

Joe always pushes to start classes because he feels that there is never enough time. "I can never think of a discussion as done; you just have to go. We're the last class out in the hallway." His kids won't leave if someone is in the middle of a sentence. Classes sometimes go into break and lunch.

Joe says that "If you don't play with them, you all sink."

The goal is not in the grade but in the process of learning. Wise teachers encourage their students to succeed.

25

History repeats itself

As the history of education is explored and analyzed, the swings of the pendulum or cycles become more and more evident. Certainly there have been many changes in the kinds of schools we create for our children over the years, but the ideal relationships of teachers to students continue to reflect former models over and over again. Wise teachers in our present society hope to lead children in democratic classrooms, but models for these can be found in the classrooms suggested by John Dewey, and models for his ideas can be found in situations that occurred in the 1800s. Throughout history the times in which learning has been student-centered have alternated with the times that learning has been teacher-centered.

Think about ways in which to integrate the philosophical pendulum that exists within yourself. Find your own happy medium or combination.

Katherine knows that her program promotes independence in actions and decision-making for children, but it includes many support systems as well. She believes that children construct knowledge in both independent and social ways. The day on which each child's own parent helps out in the classroom is usually a day spent doing all lessons with that parent in close proximity. Any parent may have anywhere from one to five children seated around him or her, but because the work is multi-task, with the assignments of each child being highly individualized, the social interactions are very much like those of a soda jerk at the counter or a blackjack dealer, not of a scout leader with a cub den. Nevertheless, frequent opportunities for incidental learning take place as the children observe the types of problems and corrections being handled by other students.

Daily, a group of four boys of different ages enjoys working and chatting together at their desks that are gathered in one corner of the room. On one day each week when Joe's grandmother, "Grandma," comes, she adds a different dynamic to their setting. She sits at a desk and works with the boys all morning, answering questions, pointing out their successes, and urging them on.

Sometimes a child ends up not working with his or her own parent at all. When being with their own moms means that some children pout, or otherwise misbehave in "at-home" ways, Katherine matter-of-factly explains that another parent will have to take over if there isn't improved cooperation. One kindergartener appears to have his mom twisted around his finger, while another kicks and hits his mom in the course of a lesson. Katherine does a lot of on-the-spot counseling, particularly at the start of the school year, in situations where Youngests are adjusting to the entire classroom situation. In other words, ABC provides support systems for parents, not just kids.

Timmy, like many others, enjoys working near his mom when she comes, but he isn't glued to her the entire time. He is comfortable in going off to do some things, like reading, independently— because, as Timmy says, he doesn't "really read yet." He is the "second one up" in this group. He likes to take a tape recorder off the shelf to listen to tapes of books in which he follows along. He has at least twenty to choose from. One choice is *Ping;* then he picks up *Bears in the Night,* by Stan and Jan Berenstain, and after a first-page cue is given by a third grader sitting nearby, he turns the pages and "reads" the entire book from memory. Then he asks an adult to read to him, choosing such titles as: *Too Much Junk Food, The Little Mouse, The Red Ripe Strawberry and The Big Hungry Bear, The Statue of Liberty, If You Give a Mouse a Cookie, Ugly Duckling, Curious George Takes a Job,* and *We're Going on a Bear Hunt.* Various children coast in and out of the informal read-aloud time, lighting on the couch to one side or the other, staying for one book or two.

Timmy's mom is glad to talk about her four children who have all gone through the program in ABC. It all began with her eldest son, who is now in eighth grade earning A's and B's and "doing great." As a preschooler, however, while he was perhaps in tune with the stories at storytime he was otherwise one of those kids who couldn't sit still. The preschool director, whose own children had come through the ABC program, recommended Katherine's class to Timmy's mom. Although she was a little nervous to have her first child in this alternative program, she is extremely pleased with its impact. She explains that it's been very different for each child, but all four of them would have been labeled as "chapter 1" or "Special Ed" in regular classrooms. The first three learned to read in second grade, fourth grade, and third grade, respectively. Katherine always reminds parents that "just as in learning to crawl and walk, children will read when they are ready. It is not going to make them better adults if they read a year or two sooner, unless someone makes it too important." She also notes that, although phonics is not explicitly taught in ABC, it is built in, to a degree. Children come to parents on the floor to get words spelled and, except for the Youngests, they are asked to think about what letters the words start with to find the places in their personal dictionaries, and they discuss which meanings and forms of the words are best for their purposes.

Timmy's mom believes that by far the most important things her children have learned in ABC are responsibility and respect. Children learn to make decisions and treat each other and their belongings with care. All of her children are doing well, and she thinks that ABC gave them time to mature and offered mobility in a safe, comfortable place.

Timmy, like all of his classmates, can find expert help if he wants or needs it. One of the two teachers or the aide will always be available, but so will half a dozen parents, and so will other kids. Sometimes another child will be the best helper, casually giving advice in words that make sense to a child's ears. Kids can get coaching with an unusual math problem or with a tricky spelling word. They can ask what a word is in a book, and they can get help finding facts.

After each school day ends, the teachers check the results of the day's work. The papers are then set out on the children's desks to begin work on the following day.

Contemplate the circle of the Tao. Understanding will come.

26

*Take your time; be attentive
and receptive*

A wise teacher learns to be a good listener. Empathy can come only from truly hearing and understanding what the student thinks. Listening does not imply agreement, nor does it require a response. Very often the students who have shared their concerns with you, who have seen your attentive gaze and nodding, sympathetic head go on to say they can do the work or solve the problem themselves.

Spend time with the students who need you to listen. You can demonstrate your acceptance of who each student is by your willingness to give of yourself. Take the time to write down (or even tape-record) what your students say and reflect upon the words at a later time. You may be surprised at what you missed upon mere listening. Few words are necessary when you listen well, and students will learn that as time goes on, they need teacher comments less and less. They will become increasingly less dependent on the teacher's approval and rely more on their own. Join the students on *their* wavelengths; your receptivity shows a weakness that ends up being a strength in winning the situation for everyone.

One of Joe's students says, "This is kind of boring right now." Other kids say, "That's rude, don't say that!" Joe asks, "Why is it boring? Now we have another topic: What is boredom? Sartre said that the death of Western civilization will be caused by freedom and boredom." Joe listens not just with his ears but also with his eyes, noticing when students seem to be troubled, often reading notes from kids. Joe explains, "We all get notes—'I'm having trouble with my brother'—notes about drug use, somebody's grandfather dies, their dog dies, some just need to write it. Very often the quiet kid will write a note: 'Will you please go over that tomorrow? I liked what you said today. Thanks.'"

Notes are a carryover from the classroom because Joe does so much listening. He tends not to give advice, but listening is interactive. He will ask specific questions or ask students what they think their options are. What do *you* think you should do? He doesn't tell them what to do. Only seldom is he the one to present the options. Joe has lunch in his room most every day; often it is to prepare for his AP class, but never does a day go by that someone doesn't stop in for a moment. James's friend Joseph is thinking of dropping out of school. He needs to hear himself talk it out.

On hectic days Joe will still listen to students, but he says things like, "Do you mind if I do this? It's Wednesday, I have to leave for my other job. Give me a few minutes or meet me down at the other building." Sometimes he asks, "Is this that important?" Some just need to get something off their chests or he'll say, "You know what, come on in."

"All right, is that it? 'Bye."

Mandy was asked to the prom by a boy who she thinks just needed someone to go with. "He doesn't call me, he doesn't talk to me, he isn't really interested in me. He's just taking me to the prom like a suitcase, just a piece of baggage." She wants to ask, "Where do I stand with you?"

After Joe came back from a Dodgers game a student named George called his home. Kids get Joe's phone number from other students even though his number is listed in the phone book. George is upset because his friends are not coming to his house to hang out. He is tired all the time. He runs himself down. His face breaks out. When he calls at eleven P.M., Joe tells George that he is lucky Joe's wife is out of town. But Joe listens.

Two sisters, former students, call to ask Joe to go to the Nixon funeral with them since it is such an historical event. A kid stops Joe in the hallway to say, "I'm turning my mother in." He means to the police. A wonderful boy, nice kid, top student. He just needs a minute to tell someone. It takes only a minute. Joe stops and listens, he doesn't keep walking. "Is that the right thing to do?" Yes. Thirty seconds. On to the next class.

According to Joe, if you let them know that you are accessible then you must be accessible. "You are obligated to be there for the kids."

You will never lose judgment if you retain calm composure.

27

Discipline yourself before
trying to discipline others

The wise teacher uses discretion, represents stability, demonstrates endurance, and maintains flexibility. Demonstrating through example is possible only if the modeling is clear. The teacher who would expect certain behaviors of her or his students can expect cooperation if those behaviors are important enough for the teacher to meet.

If you tell your children to be silent during an assembly performance, you must be silent first. If you expect punctuality from students, you must be punctual in meeting them and in returning evaluated work. If you insist upon honesty from students, you must be honest with them.

Maria finds that she gets her schoolwork done best when she does it at times that seem to be "off" to many of her colleagues. When some people rush out on a Friday, she takes off her shoes, turns on the radio, and figures that she doesn't have to be home for two and a half hours. Being able to stay in her own room, she can put things where they belong and finish the lesson planning that didn't get done the night before. She keeps a promise to herself and does not fail. The next week must be fully mapped out to pick up any appropriate books at the library, to finish replacing some of the science materials by visiting the supermarket or the drugstore. Most of what she will do will be part of her family chores and rounds, although sometimes a visit to the local lumberyard for just the right scrap wood turns out to be an adventure that she and her own children enjoy.

Saturday mornings Maria gets up late, at seven, and she sits with a steaming cup of coffee, a load of wash in the washing machine, and does something creative herself, something that will also help to make the next week's lessons more understandable. With so many new language learners in her class, she has discovered that the more pictures she can gather from magazines or draw herself, or the more tangible items she can have available, the more her kids enjoy their lessons and come away with deeper understanding. Weekends are still weekends for Maria, with family obligations and social events, but she looks forward to Mondays instead of dreading them, because she is well-prepared.

Maria knows that her colleagues hold common attitudes about how children should be. They should be polite, listen to one another, bring materials to class, treat visitors with respect, pay attention at assemblies, use the library, read a lot, do homework before TV, help other people, keep their hands to themselves in class, come to school on time, don't yell, share, be prepared.

Would it not be wise for adults to show them the Way?

28

Be humble; teach the wholeness of things

Breaking down learning into small parts can make certain types of learning more complex and less authentic. Adding the parts up again does not automatically reproduce the original, whole learning. When a concept is about to be learned, allow students to experience it in its wholeness before attempting to teach its pieces. Singing the complete song comes before learning the notes, painting a bright picture comes before studying the color wheel, hearing the total story comes before learning the words and sounds, watching the metamorphosis comes before learning its stages.

The best way to begin to understand a concept or idea is in its totality. To break a complete idea into divisions to be studied separately may prevent the entire thing from being understood or appreciated.

Expose students to wide varieties of total experiences before teaching any elements or skills.

In his Government class, Joe never talks just about Congress. He makes every attempt to show how everything is related, so students talk about the concept of government in many dimensions. Self-government: How do we use our time? How do we govern our classroom? Then: What is it like at the state level compared to the national? How about internationally? These are all in the same discussion.

In his Philosophy class Joe exclaims that holism *is* philosophy. Looking for meaning is all about wholeness. Kids might not know what the meaning of a cell is if you don't talk about the body, or the meaning of a fish if you don't talk about the river.

In Psychology, talking about society, the whole person is understood as part of something larger than the individual: the family, the culture. "If we talk about drugs, is drugs really the issue? Why is this society so addictive? In some Pacific cultures, chewing betel nut daily is no crime. Why do we get erratic, violent, depressed behaviors? We're talking about families today. Close your eyes for a minute and think silently. How does your family communicate? What is your home like?" Drawing upon prior experience, getting a sense of the whole before launching into the lesson, is so important.

And if Joe knows that he must help to create the picture, he may choose to read a short story. He knows it will work.

Be as a valley in the landscape. Your lowness will benefit you.

29

Follow the middle road;
it is the heart of knowing

Balancing the elements of various philosophies or lifestyles can be part of the way for wise teachers. They know that if all of their teaching is done with only one style, they cannot meet the varying needs of different students. The "middle road" is like the intersection of varying sets; it is not a pathway with unique properties of its own nor is it straddling a fence. The middle road allows the Tao to be versatile and allows the teacher to be whole.

Look for ways in which you can center yourself upon common features of diverse philosophies. Your own philosophy will not be eclectic; it will be pivotal, flexible.

Maria always tells people that she likes to teach. She enjoys telling other people about what she knows. She also thinks that kids enjoy telling others about things they know, so she thinks of her class as a room of teachers, a room of learners, and a place for teaching and learning to be interactive forces. Although she believes that people construct knowledge, she also thinks that classrooms come alive when some facts and information are directly shared. She promises to teach her students something new each day. She asks the children to teach her something new each day. Because many of her students are extremely knowledgeable, she finds herself using the newspaper a great deal. "Next to English, the most commonly spoken language is Spanish. Do you know what language comes next in this state of ours? What is going on in Africa? Who decides these kinds of things? Why can't they keep their agreement? Why are so many thousands of people killed? Why wasn't it on the front page?"

Kids don't always refer to the printed news for lessons, yet there is always something that Maria does not know. "No, I have never had to use the Heimlich maneuver myself. I love tamales even more now that I see how much work they take. I am shocked to find out that somebody would rob Tiny's grocery store. I am glad to hear that your sister had twins. I never knew how to stop a skateboard. I never knew the verses to that song; they're hard to hear. Now I know a lot more about Little League. No, I never took ballet—so that's what those positions are! Your cartoon should be in a newspaper. Now I understand better how electric cars work."

Maria also enjoys the ways in which literature and science enrich classroom life for her and her children. During the weeks when the tadpoles in the aquarium were turning into frogs, she made sure that there were many books about frogs around. According to Maria, the children's librarians in her town are women of wisdom and generosity. Any teacher can borrow a themed set of books to use with students, and Maria has done many book exchanges—often one whole boxful for another.

When the frog books arrived, many of the students were immediately interested in probing the different non-fiction and fiction sources for information and enjoyment. Not everyone was wild about the frogs, however. Martin was always interested in baseball, and he seldom read or wrote or talked about anything else. It seemed as if he would not become the least bit knowledgeable about frogs, and he was content to tell Maria: "Oh yeah, we did that in preschool." She explains that his comment was a surprise to her, and she worried at first that she wasn't providing enough challenge. After all, many of the books she had chosen were picture books. She had specifically gotten many levels of reading materials because of the diverse abilities of her students.

What she finally decided to do was to incorporate some direct instruction, some lessons about metamorphosis and about frogs that would be given to all of the class. What she chose to do differently, however, was to have Martin and his good friend Julian be the teachers. The lessons that the two boys taught were carefully prepared. Maria gave them advice, for she could not afford to have their talks fail. The boys took three days in school and out to gather material and prepare the charts they intended to use. They made the life-cycle stages clear. They showed the muscles of the frog and they showed the insides, what the frog looked like when it was dissected. The boys even shared a poem they had written to a tadpole.

Oh tadpole, why do you lose your tail when the days go by?
Why don't you keep it, for it would be very nice
and it would help you when you end up in a pool of water.

Maria believes that all kinds of instructional models are important to use with her students. She believes strongly in the discovery and research kinds of lessons for her students, but she also believes that there are times when the organized presentation of information can be useful, interesting, and motivating for her class. Since *she* doesn't necessarily have to be the presenter, she likes to invite appropriate guest speakers to Room 27. A biology professor came to her school to share his expertise in herpetology —the study of reptiles and amphibians—when the class frogs were developing. He had a detailed presentation about tree frogs, with photos and slides. When Dr. Cook was finished the students had dozens of questions because the tree frogs were so different from their clawed frogs.

The class, especially Martin, was full of excited questions for more than forty minutes after this talk was over.

Do not strive for extremes. In this way, solidarity is maintained.

30

Avoid using force; don't push

Effective motivation of students is not an obvious thing. Wise teachers allow children to follow their interests, then they use encouragement and natural influences to promote growth. For example, if your children want to learn more about toys, study toys. The history of toys reveals a great deal about the history of our world. Students who are pushed are not responding to their own needs and are being kept from knowing themselves and developing positive inner strength.

Ask your children what they would like to do and guide them into ways of accomplishing those things with an eye to further learnings.

Katherine has a loose structure for the topics children study and for the settings in which they work. As one child explains, "We can read wherever we want to, including *standing up.*" When the Youngers sit on the floor for group time they find places according to their peculiar habits and individual needs. They sit in various places over time, but there is never a time that they are required to sit all together as a grade-level group. The most common occurrence is that Youngers can be found on any side of the room in any one of the loose rows that form when children choose their seating. Christy likes to sit near the front, often sitting among Youngests and one or two other Youngers. Sandra may be found somewhere nearby and Karin is often several feet and individuals away. John and Joseph may be sitting anywhere from the middle to the back, but they are always together. Taylor is always toward the back because he sits with the boys who like to work together. Also Taylor's younger brother, a Youngest, is seldom far away. Philip will sit by his mom on Thursdays, but otherwise he can be found next to David, Taylor, and Bob, an Older. Dale tells me that his mom has warned him to stay away from two boys, an Older and an Oldest, so he chooses to work in other situations during personal work time, but he still chooses to sit in a threesome with them on the carpet at sharing times.

For many projects, how the children divide the labor is up to them, but most kids experience shared art and shared writing at some point. It is also almost always a reciprocal project; the students most frequently take turns doing both the drawing and the writing as they chat about what's going on. Decisions are made jointly, mostly between partners who are in the same age group. The children are also comfortable doing shared reading, and they can be found looking at books with children younger or older than they are. There are also several students who are loners, kids who would never dream of collaborating with anyone else.

Students may share the many stories that they write on one of the classroom's three Macintosh computers. Two Eldests, twin sisters who are composing a multi-chapter mystery together, ask Katherine to read a chapter to the large group. Katherine always respects the children's choices of topics. Computer stories are collected in three-ring notebooks, one for each child, that sit on shelves above the machines in the computer corner.

The newspaper is also a constant source of issues to be discussed. Katherine gets the children going. She probes the children; their answers punctuate her version of a "current events" report. She closes with, "Now we're ending a Cold War, and our words are getting warmer and warmer."

Contests of will benefit no one. Seek togetherness of spirit. When the pupil is ready the teacher will come.

31

There is no glory in victory

The teacher who wins an argument or competition does not win students over. Victory is an external event, not a personal thing. It signifies lack of harmony or understanding. A winner on one side always promotes a loser on the other. There is nothing to be proud of in any loss of humanity or humility. Full power exists only in "win-win" situations. A classroom with a "win-lose" environment is full of tension, manipulation, and one-upmanship.

If you have won a battle with your children, you have diminished their pride in thinking for themselves. Find a way for both of you to win.

Maria has a student, Corey, who wants to read comic books during SSR, Sustained Silent Reading time. Maria knows that some teachers forbid comics, whereas others are glad the child is reading *something*. It took three days before she and Corey came up with a plan. Maria never said no to him, so he kept on bringing comic books to class, but she thought about her own reasoning and shared it with Corey in private.

"Corey, I can't say no because I know comic books are interesting, and the more you read, the better you'll read. On the other hand, I want you to have a chance to read full books. They are different in their style of writing. They present ideas that aren't usually found in comics. Knowing about them will help you with your future education. Also, they aren't usually as violent as the comic books I've seen these days. Some students are not allowed to read them because they are too bloody. What do you think I should do as your teacher?"

Corey said he would figure out the answer and Maria said fine, but they would have to sign an agreement. Their new contract was for the rest of the quarter: books and comic books (tame ones) would be read. Corey continued to read comic books during the next week, but the week after that he read books at school and comic books at home, and he continued to alternate reading material over the weeks. Except when he forgot and read books two weeks in a row.

Weapons are not instruments of noble people. In the Tao, slaughter is mourned, not celebrated.

32

The Way cannot be mastered

In the Tao, the wise teacher knows that we don't "add legs to a snake." Know when to ebb in the process of teaching. Provide the essentials, light the flame, but leave the deepening of understanding to the individual. It may not happen soon, or at all, but anything the teacher pushes will be insecure at best.

Allow your children to learn from their mistakes. Allow mistakes to occur in the first place. To equate a mistake with being wrong damages the integrity of the learner and, sooner or later, of the entire class.

Joe tells his kids that one of the biggest mistakes is the fear of being wrong. "Just say something," he tells the kids. "No one is going to say something that is totally wrong." He tells them to get rid of comments like, "I'm not sure this is right." According to Joe, we put too much energy in finding answers instead of finding more questions. He feels that both teachers and students must be doing more questioning. "In many classes," according to a student, "the teacher asks the questions because he wants to see if we know the stuff." There is a difference in Joe's class. "Does anyone have a question today? Ask about the future. What kind of a president was Nixon?" Of course, there has to be a tie-in for what his kids are studying—not "How am I going to get a date for the prom?"

One day Joe holds up a cup and tells his students that he wants each of them to ask him a question about the cup. "Where did you buy it? What is in it? How do you like it? How much did it cost?" Then he asks them, "Were any of you wrong?" Asking questions about easy things always transposes into asking questions about hard things. "What would you have done if you were General Lee? Would you have done the same thing? What was the thing that motivated his choice? What if Lee's army had won?"

Joe calls on people a lot. He has a reputation. A student who is thinking of taking Joe's class next semester says, "You call on people a lot, don't you? Do you embarrass them?" Joe's belief is that if the students know that anything they say is at least partially valid, and if he gives them credit all the time for what they do say, they will speak. They shut down only if they feel put down.

He also makes a point of knowing things about students in order to build a level of comfort for them in the classroom. Aaron is a baseball freak. He thinks about everything in the context of baseball. Maria loves to dance. For Ron it's fly fishing. Joe insists that it is not crass manipulation. It isn't all relationship either. He designs his metaphors to get their attention. "You don't get their attention by demanding it or by yelling."

Joe has his students read obituaries. He feels they provide a rare time to learn about the lives of individuals. He asks, "What are some words that describe that person? Do you know anyone in your own life who is or was like this? Is there anyone who doesn't know anyone like this? How do you think that has affected you? What would you like your own obituary to say?"

No one can fully master the Way. Know when to stop.

33

*Know yourself; the influence
of virtue is immortal*

To develop inner knowledge is to gain insight. Wise teachers can see beyond the surface and make decisions that will have a positive effect upon student learning.

Keep a journal of your days at work. Reflect upon those things that went well and those that might be better. Share your process and your insights with your students. They, in turn, will share theirs with you.

Maria writes in her journal when her kids do. Initially she debated with herself, wondering if she could permit enough time out of each school day to keep a reflective journal herself. She knew that when the kids were writing she could get many of her classroom chores done, but the journaling side of her won, and she bought a notebook that was on sale at the local art supply store. It had lines for writing at the bottoms of the pages and plain white drawing spaces at the tops of the pages. Maria writes many different things in her journal. It varies by day and week. Some days she feels like writing a great deal; other days she'll write nothing at all. Some days she feels like writing stories and dreams or poetry; other days she writes lists and timelines of what has happened, just the facts. Over time, bit by bit, she has filled several different books. It brings great pleasure to Maria to reread entries and bring back memories. Sometimes she shares things with the kids, some entries that are from her personal experiences, others from shared classroom experiences: The joy she felt the morning that a horse and cow appeared near her house in a field that had long been vacant. The strange dream she had about an architecture lesson taught by the student teacher. The excitement everyone in Room 27 shared when Richard's sister delivered her baby at home the night before. The fun everyone had on their nature walk to the rocky riverbed. The day Room 27 sold its artwork to the rest of the school at noon, and made thirty-seven dollars for its art fund. The day her class paid a visit to the local convalescent home and how all the class worried about the eighty-year-old woman who whined, "Mommy, I want to go home."

Some entries are just for fun, like Maria's plans for her colleagues to form a group to enter the famous Doo-Dah Parade as the Precision Chalk and Eraser Team, the Dunce Caps, the Bar Graphs, the If-Thens, or the Chalk Boreds. And she saves the funny things that her own children said, like the day five-year-old Park was finishing the alphabet song, and sang, "Now I've killed my ABCs, aren't you very proud of me?" Or when he was upset that his dad forgot his toy bag, and out of the blue yelled, "Swine!" Or when Cara tried counting: ". . . ten, eleven, twelve, thirteen, nexteen, twenty."

Because Maria has kept journals for a long time, she sees that some years are different from others. One year she tried very hard to remember her dreams and it turned out that her greatest success came after she woke up and went back to sleep for an extra half hour. She could write down a quick sentence at home and then write the rest of the details during their early morning journal time when she got to school. Some of her dreams about school were not so pleasant. In one dream she was teaching the children the song, "Up, Up and Away," and, one by one, they started to dance on their desks and she could not get them down. "We can't sing if you don't cooperate," she admonished. "Desks are not for dancing." She tried all of her management tricks to no avail. Luckily the dream ended before she lost all patience.

Another year she focused on writing funny stories and anecdotes and she began to see the humor in all kinds of scenes and situations around her. Embarrassing moments emerged as one of the themes. She once went shopping with a friend who kept on popping out of the dressing room at the store to seek her opinion about various shirts. Upon seeing her friend in one white, open-necked blouse, Maria told her not to get that one because it made her neck look long and skinny. Her friend had replied, "But, Maria, this is the blouse I wore coming here!"

This year she wanted to concentrate on moments and adventures in nature and the pleasure they give her. Maria has written about hummingbirds in the *Birds of Paradise,* the horned owl who watched her from a rooftop one dawn, pine trees humming in winter waves of air as she passed on her cross-country skis, walking along a dry stream bed in the mountains to find rocks that were worn into smooth organic shapes that felt good in her hand, searching for seashells on a misty morning, walking up and down dry hills to come across the foundation of a building long gone and making up a story of what might have been there.

Whatever the time or the topic, the kids are always interested in what Maria writes when they do. Maria usually doesn't encourage the kids to write to a specific topic at any point. She does, however, answer their questions when they want to know what she is going to write. This year there are journals full of nature writing in Room 27; Maria's is just one.

To know others is to be wise. To know oneself is to be enlightened.

34

Do not strive for greatness

When the wise teacher is least insistent, greatness will come. Success is entwined with the progress of students and they will thrive under subtle, albeit high, expectations.

Center your motives upon making your students the best that they can be. A high-quality environment will bring forth high-quality achievement.

Children have free access to all of the materials in the ABC classroom—multitudes of interesting puzzles, books, manipulables, art supplies, games, and tools that are boxed and clearly labeled, sitting on designated shelves in various parts of the room so that things may be found by all, adults and children.

Katherine's collection of books rivals that of a school library. In addition to the step-shelves and wire revolving racks of books that surround students who sit on the two couches in the "library" section of the room, there are shelves and shelves of books that surround the library and further shelves that wander around the classroom. Books are plentiful and easy to find. One special bookcase is known as Adrienne's Bookcase; it holds over one hundred hardcover picture books that deal with sensitive topics and have been donated to ABC over the years in memory of Adrienne, a young family member of a former ABC student. A rolling wooden cart holds books beneath an unabridged dictionary. Special groups of books are neatly organized in cardboard boxes on shelves beneath windows and across the back wall of one classroom. Boxes hold sets such as *The Animal Kingdom Encyclopedia, The Ocean World of Jacques Cousteau, Eyewitness Books, Value Tales, Childcraft,* all of the Dr. Seuss books, sets of "Read Together" beginner books. In other parts of the room books stand supported against half-walls across the back edges of tables that also serve as desks for many children. Books can be found almost everywhere in the classroom, on tables and shelves, except in the many places that hold other special materials.

Math and science materials are grouped into hundreds of cardboard boxes that are reinforced with tape and clearly labeled with black ink on white paper. Unifix cubes and pattern blocks, checkers and chess, Monopoly and Rig-a-jig-jig, spinners and coin stamps, ten sticks and hundred blocks, tangrams and math jewels, beans and buttons, magnifiers and corks, rulers and protractors are just some of the items in marked boxes near several open work spaces throughout the brown-carpeted rooms.

Katherine's efforts over the years—asking for materials instead of textbooks from her administration, suggesting that parents provide lasting "gifts," finding book sales and community donors —have paid off. And like so many teachers, her own investment of money has made a difference as well.

Do not insist upon making claims for yourself; greatness will come to you.

35

The Way has its own rhythm;
use it

Individuals who are engaged in what they are highly, intrinsically motivated to do end up losing track of time and can go for hours without getting tired. When activities go on to their natural finish points, bells and imposed ending times won't be needed. The Tao permits a tireless state for teacher and student.

You will want to get lost in your work.

The students in Katherine's class know that if they want to, they can read six books in a row at one sitting. Or they can write a story that is six feet long and takes three days to write, if they like. Time is flexible in this multi-age classroom, and although each child is expected to do reading, math, and writing every day, any child may alter that pattern by writing a note of explanation to Katherine. When a child is deeply involved with a project, time goes by in unusual ways. Katherine does not believe in cutting the day up into subjects like science and social studies, nor does she think that an important project must yield to a set schedule. She sees blocks of time existing over days as useful for some projects.

GRETA K. NAGEL

When several ABC students decided to write pieces for Peace Day at Lemon School, they were consumed with creating pictures and working on various drafts of poems. For two days, their time was invested deeply into thoughts and expressions of peace. They found books and reference entries about peace and awards and peace movements and peace organizations. They read books and articles about famous people who were devoted to peace. They studied a famous painting, *The Peaceable Kingdom*. And they talked about peace with each other, with several parents, and with Katherine as well. Their poems contained rich language and provocative ideas, and when the children, all Eldests at the ages of eight and nine years old, stood to read their work for the large group gathering, many children and adults were truly moved to tears.

Swim with the current; its uses are limitless.

36

*The weak and the tender overcome
the hard and the strong*

Wise teachers know that yielding can win over an aggressor. They do not attempt to do the impossible, but turn strength into weakness with caution, reservation, flexibility, sincerity, and honesty. Powerful fish swim in deep waters.

Be willing to meet a strong or difficult adversary on his or her own ground. Admit your own mistakes with honesty, and allow the other to "set the hook" through his or her own aggression.

Joe rambles on one day. "I have a thing about troublemakers. Other teachers ask, 'What do you do to keep him under control? He's just a jerk, that's all.'" To Joe, these are the very kids who respond and make things interesting. For example, Jonas drives other teachers crazy. He has a world view that he is the one who determines the stories the class will share. He sits next to someone new every day. "I try to get kids like Jonas to be leaders in class. Isaac was the only kid I had to take aside: 'I know sometimes you have trouble with teachers. Can you relax?' I talked to him during seventh period, you know, end of the day.

"Isaiah? He just talks, he yells, he bumps people, a seventeen-year-old. He blurts out inappropriate comments, but he doesn't use profanity. The kids like him even though he bothers them. I made him a leader of a group. He has a lot of energy. By the way, he is a terrific drummer. He wants to be a rock and roll artist. He *loves* it. I allude to drumming in the course of teaching when he's there. He creates tension, but he is the one who makes some of the decisions, pushing things forward. His group did a wonderful job."

According to Joe, Caleb is the most aggressive one. He hits his fist into his palm all the time. He is sure that Caleb thinks Joe doesn't like him. And Joe is always thinking of a way to proceed that includes Caleb. Joe believes that as soon as he says, "All right, that's it, you've got detention," it will kill learning for Caleb. Joe explains that teachers are not aggressive by nature, but they are threatened by aggression in students, and they don't know how to respond—but if students are treated right they can become learners and leaders. They really do need to get "stuff" out of their systems. Aggressors are very emotional; those who deal with them successfully are unemotional. They don't lose their cool.

What is more powerful than water? It pulverizes rock into sand, yet it is supple, yielding.

37

Seek simplicity and honor what is known

Wise teachers are interested in the questions, skills, and knowledge already held by students. They become the springboards for future endeavors.

Ask students to tell you through writing and discussions about the things they have already learned and what they wonder about. Build upon their answers in shared planning for the future.

In ABC, children often share experiences and special belongings with the large group. Children bring in toys and animals and stories of recent events in their families. Children share when they choose to, usually asking permission of Katherine the day before. Sharers represent all the age levels in ABC. When the class was following newspaper accounts of an art exhibit of giant umbrellas that was installed in the desert, they discussed the aesthetics of the event and they shared the tragedy of the deaths of a workman and tourist that occurred when some of the umbrellas collapsed in the wind. Several children who were going to drive to the desert to see the giant umbrellas had their trip cancelled because the mother who was driving became very sick. The children stood before their classmates and told of their feelings about the exhibit and their feelings about being disappointed in their plans.

On another day, a student brought in a page from a circular and shared a picture of their classmate, a Younger girl from ABC who modeled clothes for a local department store's flyers. A brother and sister who had just adopted a desert tortoise brought it to class in an aquarium and elaborated on its care and handling and on how the animal was obtained in a legal adoption from an egg of a captive tortoise. The brother and sister also set up the rules for the other children to follow when they observed the turtle that day.

The large-group time also involves children in much of the rulemaking in ABC and informs them about social occurrences and how they have been handled. When one Youngest boy had not yet learned to sit still during carpet time, the children were involved in an objective discussion of what to do. The child remained anonymous, but the class helped determine that children who don't sit still must go to their seats and do not get to participate in group time, even if it is a birthday celebration day. The exception would be if it is the person's own birthday, then he or she would get to participate and pass out birthday treats as usual. When one child had ignored a "See Katherine" disc on her paper for days the children were brought in on the frustration of a teacher being ignored—and learned that they had a teacher who would wait it out just to see when this person would handle the problem herself.

Internal growth comes from practicing simplicity in living and work.

38

*Virtue is its own reward;
differences arise when the Way is
lost*

Wise teachers expect to be trusted to continue their hard work. They do not expect to be given status or wealth. They are examples of intrinsic motivation at its best, for when something must be done it gets done without special reward. Teaching is by itself a reward in the minds of the best teachers. A good day means that learning is taking place; good teachers anticipate tomorrow with excitement and a sense that the work is worth the effort.

Do not expect compensation for the many facets of your work that you must accomplish as a teacher. Once you accept a position with its related pay, do what you must to get the job done well. You will wear many hats—including that of lifelong learner.

Joe knows that teaching is more than a mere job or profession. It is also about helping young people to create and fulfill dreams. He went to his mailbox where there was a letter from Africa, a surprise out of the blue. Karina, a former student from four years ago, now lives in Ghana and wrote him a thank-you. "You have come into my thoughts many times since arriving in Ghana. Maybe it's because you were one of the few people who had faith in me and knew that indeed one day I would plant my feet somewhere in this vast continent's soil . . ." And it ends: "Thank you so much for your faith in me. When others laughed at my dreams and my goals, you were there to say 'right on.' That has meant a great deal to me in the pursuit of those dreams and goals."

Joe says that he never knows where it all leads or what it all means. The senior class officers have asked him to read the list of graduates at graduation and the student body officers have asked him to chaperone dances. A single student wants help with a problem, parents ask him to give the eulogy at the funeral of their son who was killed by a drunk driver. A former student invites him to her wedding, another to the christening of her newborn son. In another town, one of Joe's students accepts a scholarship from a charitable organization. She gives a brief speech and names Joe as the teacher who helped her to see what was important in life.

To Joe, teaching comes with rewards and blessings far different from, and more meaningful than, scores on the printout from the standardized test.

Hold the Way with conscience and do not expect a response.

39

Oneness, not fragmentation

Wise teachers find ways to relate different learnings to a common theme. A study of whales, for example, is not just a lesson in science. Speaking, reading, and writing about the whales incorporate the language arts; studying their songs involves music; drawing or painting them or making models of them incorporates the visual arts; studying their relative sizes and weights entails math; the history of their killings is part of social studies. Within a science classroom an English teacher can monitor students' written lab reports. Students will therefore share the excitement of their discoveries, which may go beyond the immediately apparent focus of their study.

Find ways to web learnings with a common focus or theme. You will increase eagerness in your students and create natural motivations for them to explore and perform various tasks. Their investigations, not yours, will bring respect to your program. Humility on your part enables unity in the classroom.

When Maria decided that their theme for the semester could be the radio, she was excited about the many ways her kids could help to create the learning opportunities as they went. There were some things that she knew would happen as the children wrote their programs for station KIDS: children with various talents in areas such as singing, cooking, sports, politics, rock, drama, or science could be motivated to look up information to create their shows. Putting on the shows, several a day, was also part of their language arts. The most surprising event was when Irene, a very shy girl, went into the "radio" to do her show, and after her own brief introduction of herself, began to sing "God Bless America" and another song in a strong, beautiful voice. Everyone looked at each other in astonishment.

The funniest show was when Richard got behind the box and did a show about visiting interesting restaurants in the area. As the restaurant host, he went in to interview each owner about the menu and prices. Richard played each owner as well, and as "The Restaurant Show" went from Italian, to Japanese, to Mexican, to German, and then to Greek establishments, he adjusted the owners' accents accordingly. Some kids didn't believe that it could all be Richard.

In science, the class studied how radios work and learned about radio waves. With the help of one boy's father, a group of students built their own radio transmitter. Another group read a book, *Today I Am a Ham*, and learned how to become ham operators. The local ham radio association sent over two men to talk to the kids and share their equipment van. The class also had permission to use the two-way radios that the principal and the custodian usually used.

In social studies, kids drew pictures of the appearances of radios since their beginnings with Marconi in 1895. They learned how the radio played into many famous events, such as helping in the rescue of the *Titanic* survivors. They studied the kinds of programs that were popular since Enrico Caruso sang opera in 1910, especially during the so-called golden age of broadcasting that occurred between 1925 and 1950.

Listening to the real radio was seen as a special treat in Maria's classroom. Listening to tapes of old radio shows was also a lot of fun. One family shared a set of tapes from a children's show that had been popular in the early 1950s. Each student also adopted a radio station, and assumed its call letters as his or her pseud-onym. The local FM station invited the class to visit their studio.

And for a month Room 27 was allowed to do a short radio broadcast of school news over the Riverview School intercom three mornings a week.

To achieve oneness is to be fulfilled.

40

Something comes from nothing;
nothing comes from something

Wise teachers recognize that the interactions of polarities will help promote learning in the classroom. Tension must accompany learning and students must have opportunities to disagree and find resolutions to their differences: "You can't have life without death."

Permit students to see opposing viewpoints on issues. In understanding one, they can better understand the other.

When Joe has second period Mike, a big red-faced athlete, sits on top of his desk. He gets really bothered by things. His face gets deeper red. He is the kid who is turning his mother in for drug abuse. "Like caning in Singapore . . . maybe if we had more of that." Joe turns to Michelle, who is very proper and dainty. She sits with her hands folded. "What do you think about that? What is the proper role of government?" The class knows how quiet she is. The class quiets down when she speaks. She says that punishment never works. The child learns fear or becomes sneaky, trying to get away with things. Mike says, "What are you going to do, turn all the kids loose?" And Michelle replies, "Why not have parents do that? Or have 'punishment places'?" She is incensed at the position Mike has taken. After her reply she sits while Mike retorts. They both end up listening and saying "I understand" after five minutes of going back and forth. At the resolution, integrity intact, no one has won. Joe says that if there is no hostility, that is a sign that a class has gone well.

Joe says to notice how people walk out of a classroom. That tells pretty much how it went.

While Michelle sits, Mike speaks. While Mike sits, Michelle speaks. So the Way is followed.

41

Appearances can deceive

Wise teachers do not give up. They recognize that sometimes students may appear to be making little progress, but they do not give up the Tao for methods that have the appearance of quick learning. Generations of students who take years of history and forget it all because it was rote memorization of names and dates, or those who take years of foreign language classes and can't speak or write, tell us that it would be better to encourage learning deeply through many activities that apply acquired skills and knowledge.

Do not be fooled into thinking that rote learning and the rewards of temporary high test scores will make for lifelong retention and caring. Do what your insight tells you to do in terms of helping students to experience learning.

Maria believes that the more her students read and the more they know about interesting subjects, the better they will be able to perform on tests. She makes one part of her program synchronize specifically with standardized tests, and that is to have the kids come up with sample test questions each day. The students on the committee ask the rest of the kids one math question and one reading question a day. Then she has all the kids organize themselves into small teams to turn the questions into multiple-choice questions with good distractors. She believes that the conversations about the distractors help students clear up some of their misconceptions about the various concepts, and that the time is well spent compared to the experience of responding to a question posed by a book or by the teacher.

The Way is known through intuition and tireless practice.

42

*Harmony is to be achieved through
the blending of the passive and the
active—the* yin *and the* yang

Wise teachers learn to balance activities that require gathering, sharing, and analyzing information in linear ways *(yang)* with activities that involve creativity, emotional expression, and personal insight *(yin)*. Students will gain from having both types of experiences.

Do not hesitate to provide information through directed lessons, but always recognize the need for students to construct their own meanings and organize ideas for themselves through creative experiences.

Katherine invites many individuals, both parents and outsiders, to speak to the children in ABC. When Magic Johnson contracted the HIV virus the concern was great, and Katherine had one of the moms, someone who is also a parenting workshop teacher, come to talk with the children. Her message is not delivered as a professional with clinical facts to relate but as a mom who, before she was married and had her daughter, once lived with a roommate, a homosexual man, who later developed AIDS. With tears in her eyes, she talks about a large, strong, intelligent friend who lost one hundred pounds, becoming weaker and weaker to die as a withered impression of his former self. She also speaks about how difficult it was for her five-year-old daughter to go with her to see this very sick individual and wonders out loud if it was the right decision to bring her daughter to visit him. The adults present, through their own tears, can consider how different and human this tale is from the sensational stories of the popular basketball star that filled the front pages of the newspapers at the time.

The children from all grade levels ask the mother many specific questions about her friend and the effects of his disease. Katherine signals her approval of the mom's honest but purposely sketchy descriptions of how body fluids shouldn't be shared and how working and going to school with infected individuals is safe. When a third grader asks just how did Magic get the virus, the mother's eyes connect with Katherine's and Katherine cautiously explains that "he wasn't careful with his health practices." Katherine later reflects how grateful she is to have read those words in a newspaper.

There is a sophistication in the level of the topics that are broached in ABC, but parents and teachers avoid pushing the boundaries of what might be considered developmentally inappropriate information for their children. There was, for example, no talk of condoms and safe sex.

Parents also often come with special projects that the children can do if they sign up. Splash art and cooking, drawing and crafts, things that require special materials and close-at-hand direction, often take place in the table area by the southwest door. The activities are not for everyone. Kids sign up only if they are interested. Nevertheless the opportunity is there, and parents and relatives have a chance to share talents and interests. The small groups are not usually constructed of any one age group; group compositions are mixed. The purpose of the times are not for cooperative activities, but rather are creative opportunities for children to do independent things side by side. One popular activity was making fish prints. A parent brought in fish from the fish market, and under her guidance, students inked one side of a fish and carefully made prints that were artistically lovely and scientifically fascinating to everyone.

When Katherine meets with the large group each day, she highlights special pictures and stories that she has selected from the children's work. She emphasizes her intrigue with thought-provoking ideas and interesting words and sentence patterns, using pauses and rising intonations of her voice as she reads. One day she shows five paintings of trees, all of them managing to avoid the "lollipop" look that children often use, all appearing to have the individuality of reality, with imaginatively colorful skies created through a variety of brushes or sponges and strokes that create different textures. A great deal of "indirect-direct" instruction occurs in the large-group setting. Chats about techniques and specific information grow out of the contexts of the children's work.

Children easily learn what things are important to Katherine. Her primary interest is in quality of thought within writing, not quantity and not initial correctness. Mistakes are to be corrected, but they are made; grownups make them too. Life is full of problems to be solved, and this theme permeates many large-group meetings. Not only are problems common, but the pain and sadness they cause are very real events, and the ways in which people deal with their troubles provide important lessons. There is jubiliation in overcoming adversity. Adults visit as guests, sometimes as honored celebrities, as in the case of pitcher Dave Dravecky who lost his arm to cancer. Sometimes the guest is someone with something to teach or share, as in the case of the dad who is an artist, the mom who is a storyteller.

Harmony is a group project.

43

Use your resources

Not only does the wise teacher model behaviors and show concepts through hands-on lessons, but examples of ideas and products that are done by other students can become very important parts of the classroom. Children learn from one another. The writings of other children are not just for hanging on the bulletin board. They can become important parts of the classroom and school libraries. Visual and auditory resources, organized to be easily accessible, set important examples for students. Pictures and charts that demonstrate concepts and provide useful information can become part of the room environment. Tapes that children have made—of stories that might be difficult for some children to read on their own, of explanations that use children's language to provide "how to" information—can be part of an audio library.

Create a classroom that is a resource center with accessible materials in order for children to take charge of their own learning. If you provide the materials, you are influencing a large part of the learning as well.

Groups of students, in turn, should be encouraged to build resource centers for other classes, for the school library, and even for district-level learning centers. This way students will learn that they are not only targets for academic "delivery systems," but that they are also valued as authors in resource acquisition and development.

Joe has his students do a lot of reactive writing. He tries to teach by example, using writings of other students. His kids regularly read what they write out loud. One final end-of-semester activity is to have each student write a letter to the whole class and then read it aloud. Some write to several individuals or to just one person. Many give just a general "farewell address."

Wordless teaching is attained by few. This is the ultimate.

44

Keep a sense of balance

Teachers know that the multiple tasks of running a rich program can be endless. They set limits to their work day and work week, looking to many expert teachers who, although part of their work hours are flexible, often work a fifty-hour week. Knowing that they work best in the mornings or evenings, wise teachers set aside those hours to plan and gather resources. Priorities of health or family must not be lost to work, nor should work suffer because of excessive personal commitments.

Decide your personal limits and prioritize the things that you must, and want, to do. Always reward yourself with things you want to do when you have accomplished things you must do.

Maria knows that some work days are longer than others. Meetings are scheduled, both before and after school. Sometimes she has meetings after meetings and she doesn't get home until several hours after school. Because she treasures her moments with her children at home, she saves certain family times for everyone to get together and she makes "appointments" and "dates" with her son and daughter so she can spend time with them on days that are not so jam-packed with school commitments. Some times involve both of her children, others may be spent with just one. Some occasions are very simple, like driving down Jacaranda Street when the trees are in bloom, or stopping for a Coke at a local walk-in restaurant. Sometimes they involve errands, and the excursions become a combined visit to the comic-book store after the cleaning is picked up from the cleaners, or to the museum when the new school shoes have been bought. Sometimes it means eating dinner out, just child and parent together, with no other family members present.

Maria is also pleased to live near such special neighbors. They are treasures to her. In order to find time to see each other more, she made a promise to her next-door neighbor to roll out of bed at five-thirty on three mornings a week. They walk and discuss the children and laugh about the local neighborhood animals who watch them from the tops of cars and behind fences. It saves her the money she was spending at the local fitness center. Her half-hour hikes have gained her the pleasure of laughing and chatting with her dear neighbor as well as helping her to stay in shape.

Seek contentment. In this way you will benefit others.

45

Tranquility is more important than perfection

An agitated, irritated teacher cannot be effective. The wise teacher finds ways to become an example of tranquility, incorporating quiet moments of reflection or meditation into the day. Wise teachers do not find the time, they make the time and recognize that something else may not be perfect. However, usefulness is not impaired by imperfection; you can drink from a chipped cup.

Set aside the moments for activities that will help you to center and find emotional tranquility.

In Katherine's room some of the things that happen are part of a low-anxiety, low-stress environment for everyone. One focus for a daily whole-class activity is the free, expressive movement that students do to various pieces of music each afternoon. Katherine will start a tape or record that varies in theme with topics that have come up, or with a particular holiday that is near, or with a mood or a request of one of the class members. The children— and any adults who care to participate—may walk and prance, dip and twirl, and use arm movements or not, according to their individual preferences. They may stay in one area or travel across the space of the double classroom as they choose. Some may want to follow each other to do a dance that is similar, or some may even model known dances like "La Raspa" for other students who want to learn the steps. The movement time is a free-choice time for everyone in terms of how to move. The only requirement is that they engage in movement.

Another common event occurs during times on the carpet for some children, mostly girls, as they listen. It is "doing" someone else's hair. With fingers or an occasional small comb students engage in smoothing, parting, braiding, twisting, banding, combing, fluffing, and patting the strands of one another's hairdos. Sometimes only one person will be busy, sometimes two girls may arrange one head of hair, and there are even times when a small train of girls will be engaged in fixing the hair of the next one. This sort of social touching extends across age groups, and because it is not frowned upon by the adults it becomes a part of the large-group scene, usually not at the first morning meetings but at late-morning and afternoon gatherings. The hairdo activity is friendly and comfortable, and the children listen and speak as part of the attentive group, in spite of their busy handwork.

Katherine maintains for herself one time of the day as sacred— her lunch hour. She creates an invisible shield around herself, even though she often spends her lunch time physically in the classroom and in close proximity to children and parents. They know that this is her time.

Peace and quiet help set the world right.

46

Be content with contentment

Wise teachers learn that there are joys to be found in the simple pleasures of life. Friendships, reading, music, and enjoyment of nature can bring lifelong joy. Adventures need not be in expensive or exotic places, for lavish desires may create only feelings of longing or jealousy.

Finding the simple aspects of life that give you pleasure is a task that will pay you over and over again.

On the wall in Joe's classroom is a poster that reads "Live simply, so that others may simply live." Joe likes to share stories about the lives of simple people. Often it is by way of anecdotes or aphorisms. He also thinks that stories are important. The daily newspaper is a common source of information and inspiration, and Joe reads aloud about people who have simplified their lives, or about people who live simply and use their energies to lead people-conscious and environmentally conscious lives. The stories that he finds are not page-one news, but with a few turns of the pages, he is able to share some hopeful ideas about the world. A woman who works to help kids in her neighborhood, a man who gave up his work as a corporate CEO to work for global understanding, an eighty-year-old woman who goes out daily to turn on showers, prepare food, clean house and help a dozen elderly friends and acquaintances live out their lives in their own homes. At other times the stories he tells are about his own friends and acquaintances: the retired couple who take walks together and pick up trash along the way each morning, the adults and teenagers who deliver meals to shut-ins each day, the young people who work at the hospital or with the Scouts.

Joe likes simple pleasures himself and his students sense this, although he doesn't talk about it much. He takes walks daily and he loves to read. Besides reading two newspapers, he subscribes to seven magazines that he skims for interesting items. He does yoga and he spends time daily in contemplation. He also has a wide range of tastes in music, from Beethoven and Mozart to the Grateful Dead and Motown. He even likes the "Top 40" that his own children listen to at home. Joe also enjoys conversation. He meets with a group of men his own age monthly for coffee, bagels, and muffins and fresh fruit for three or four hours of conversation ranging from world affairs to personal issues. He and his wife belong to a "couples group," where they enjoy a potluck dinner with five or six other couples and then spend the evening conversing on issues about lifestyles, communication, men and women, politics.

He also prefers short three- or four-day trips to long, complicated ones with sophisticated itineraries and plans. He loves being home with his family. They usually eat supper together and talk about things of interest to them all. He and his son love baseball, and on a warm summer evening he would just as soon be at the local college or professional stadium in a general-admission seat with a diet Coke and a bag of peanuts. Baseball to Joe is the simplest of sports, made more dramatic by the fact that there is no clock. His students tell him that his is the only classroom on campus without a clock on the wall. He likes it that way. For years he never wore a watch, but he decided to buy one from a varsity baseball player during the team's fund-raiser. He wears it so he won't start a discussion topic in class near the end of the period.

Fools are avaricious. There is no "beyond contentment."

47

Cultivate inner knowledge

Wise teachers develop insight. They know that they do not have to go far to learn wisdom, and they know to stay close to situations in order to clarify what's going on. Individuals who become sensitive to others and learn to understand students' motivations can be very powerful teachers. They take care to question and think about the effects of their words and actions. They are also secure enough to ask for feedback from both students and fellow teachers. They learn and grow from these responses.

Reflection does not require that you go any farther than your door. Learn to spend time thinking instead of "running around."

At the end of each day Joe sits at his desk in the quiet to think back about the various periods of the day. "I probably let Jeremy talk too much today in second period. I should have started the discussion with Amy. Seventh period was full of too many arguments." Daily self-reflection, for just a few minutes, is one piece of how Joe thinks about revisions and adjustments to his courses. He also stops every once in a while to ask the class members how they are doing, how in their opinion he is doing, and what changes need to be made. "You talk too fast." "You talk too much." "You are in such a hurry to make your point that sometimes you interrupt students." "Let's not do a Philosophy reading every day." When Joe gets going he sometimes goes too fast too far. Sometimes his behaviors contradict the goals that he holds so dear. He appreciates being reminded of this.

Joe keeps a journal, not in a book but as a collection of thoughts in a manila envelope by his easy chair at home and in his desk at school. When he jots down a reflection about the day or ideas for tomorrow, small pieces of paper get slipped into the envelope. Joe thinks that his best ideas have come to him when he was involved with yoga or when he takes walks in the evening.

He also asks his students, in one or two writing assignments, to share anything personal that might affect how they do in the class. Share an idea that is the most profound for you and tell why. When a student is willing to share this idea out loud, a real leap of faith and trust can take place in the classroom. When Joe passes out a midterm with six essay questions, he tells his students, "Take five minutes to read the questions. See what you think about them." Joe asked three questions that the students thought were redundant, and as he listens, he comes to agree. Joe reworks the midterm exam, retypes and runs it off again. The questions don't get any easier but the test gets better. In addition to the questions Joe asks, he has each student come up with a question that is important to him or her and answer it.

Finals are not just written tests; they become a series of events that may last an entire week. This year is the final dinner where students have to share in the style of a meeting of the minds. Socrates will have to wear a robe. The students talk about it fondly as "The Last Supper." Built into Joe's written exam are a couple questions about how he taught the class—his style, use of resources, fairness in grading, mistakes he made, what were the great moments in the class, and what changes are needed.

Joe is not a big fan of training or staff development unless it is offered by his own school. He has taken three formal classes in twenty-four years. He will go to a conference if there is something specific he wants to get out of it or if he can go with someone he knows in order to bounce ideas around. It is stimulating, but he does not go from workshop to workshop. He does not enjoy taking time away from school if it means missing his classes. Besides, conferences are very expensive. His angle is, "What I need to do is to promote growth by thinking about what's happening with my students. Two weeks ago my two psychology classes were dead. I said to them, 'I'm sensing boredom. Are you stuck? Am I stuck? What do you need?'" Joe finds growth in working through the ongoing predicaments and recognizing the successes.

Oftentimes the farther one travels, the less one knows.

48

The pursuit of the Way is not
like the pursuit of information

Learning is increased by effort day by day, but growing in the Tao means decreased effort. The wise teacher learns to work in effortless ways, doing things that come without stress. At the end of a good day he or she might say something like, "I don't know, everything just seemed to flow."

Teach by doing what comes naturally. If you wish to change your ways, make sure that the decision is yours and that your students will be the ones to benefit. They will let you know.

Katherine knows that her daily contact with parents is useful for getting most problems straightened out. When Jane, an Older, twists the truth over the course of a few days, Katherine takes the opportunity to discuss things with her dad outside the classroom door on the day he comes to ABC. For a first-grader like Philip choices are enhanced on the day when his mom is there. Philip would not have been admitted to this class without his parents' commitment. Like all parents who have children in this "alternative" nongraded primary classroom, one adult from the family is expected to work on the floor in the classroom for three hours each week. Only parents with very rare work situations, as is the case with a woman who teaches fourth grade in a nearby district, take on other ABC jobs like volunteer coordinator. Being "on the floor" is both literal and figurative in ABC, for a great deal of children's work is indeed done on the floor and most parents sit and work on the carpet, resting against special backrests in order to be accessible to the children.

As Katherine explains, parents bring children to ABC for a variety of reasons. Some are too immature to enter "regular" first grade. Many have brothers and sisters who are or have been in ABC. One is too academically bright to remain in a regular kindergarten. One has been suspended twice and almost expelled from another school setting. Most parents have been seeking for their children this room full of opportunity for choice and independence. The children are not all from the Lemon School attendance area; the majority have transferred to Lemon in order to participate in this alternative program. Half of the students are from other neighborhoods in the same school district and the rest are from an assortment of seven surrounding school districts. Information about this class spreads by word of mouth to people who are dedicated to their children's education. There is usually something unusual about their child's adjustment in other settings and there is something unusual about ABC.

Within the immediate Lemon School community, some parents of neighborhood children are skeptical and they don't feel that it is really effective. Katherine's classroom has "a rainbow of races and cultures," but, as she says, she would like to have further diversity yet. Because Katherine's program is not overly publicized, neighborhood parents and a lot of the teachers who work at the same school say, "Education isn't like this." Katherine has heard it all before. She and her aide of twenty-two years have lived through a great deal—mostly being ignored or having people say bad things about them and their "strange" ideas. The program has been called "dogmatic," or "for smart kids" and "for parents who don't have anything better to do," in an "overprotective atmosphere." But even knowing many of the criticisms, Katherine continues to maintain an unusual program that has been dearly loved by many and is cherished by a growing number of people at present. Community members and colleagues in other schools point out that ABC has something to offer to an educational scene where real change is difficult to find. Katherine has worked closely with her kids and their parents to make adjustments over the years, but she maintains an unwavering and deep commitment to children as choicemakers. She knows that they will learn by doing.

The Way is a powerful force. If it did not draw criticism it would not be the Way.

49

Regard the students' ideas with respect and treat everyone with goodness and honesty

Wise teachers learn not to be judgmental. They do not respond to their students by telling them they are wrong. They do not put down students, no matter who they are—instead they use words that can accept students' misguided ideas or inappropriate answers and ask for the thinking behind them. They can tell students that they have just provided the answer to the next question, or they can ask students to clarify opinions and facts. Wise teachers are patient. Even a "smart" remark can be accepted and shown to be a useful remark, if only the context were different. In the Tao teachers do, however, know to express displeasure if students transgress their *own* rules for fairness and politeness.

Learn to use students' ideas. Your acceptance will promote the risk-taking that allows them to become creative and critical thinkers.

If one of her children ever answers a question with "I don't know," Maria sees that as her problem, not the child's, for she has asked a poor question by asking for something too specific or she has simply asked the wrong child. She wants her kids to feel free to talk, and she wants them to meet success so that they won't stop. She designs her questioning with care, and she aims to allow all children the success of giving "correct" answers. She also designs her responses, and has even said on occasion things like: "Jan, your answer is correct if I had only asked the question, 'When did the Egyptians *begin* building the pyramids?' " Most of the time she asks questions that elicit the kids' experiences or their opinions, and as long as students back them up, things are fine.

One day when she asked the students if they thought the ancient Egyptians' concept of the afterlife reminded them of any other beliefs, she had the students carry on a conversation that lasted fifteen minutes before she said another word. She was pleased with herself for not interjecting anything, and she was delighted with the interesting comparisons and contrasts that students brought up. Sometimes, Maria even rests one hand over her mouth as she sits with her students, a silent reminder to herself that her words are not always so important.

Make the minds of your students your own.

50

A person who does not strive
intensely after life nor tangle with
danger can preserve life well

Wise teachers choose their courses to fit their personalities. What may be too intense for one person can be a normal opportunity for another. The teacher who suffers from burnout is often one who did not know to choose personal priorities well. Rest, exercise, and reaching out to others are important for all. The constant decision-making of teaching creates pressures that can be compared to air traffic control, minus only the ever-present specter of life-or-death situations. Nevertheless, danger does emerge for teachers because of violence from within the school and from without in the form of intruders. The wise teacher does not fight danger with aggression. In the Tao, subtle ways win.

Learn to relax from the tensions of your constant pressures as a teacher. Use the Tao in situations of potential conflict.

Katherine has always maintained an open-door policy in ABC, and many people have come from other school districts throughout the region to see her class in action. However, a phenomenon that often happens to people who are "different," either because they are of an uncommon culture/belief system or are of a different era or ahead of their time, has occurred in Katherine's classroom. Appreciation for the ABC program stems from distant places. Nevertheless, she has consistently made choices that will benefit the ABC program. She has avoided or ignored many political tides, and it is fortunate that many of her beliefs and practices are consistent with the frameworks, research, and policies that will lead educators into the twenty-first century.

Running a program with so much emphasis on hands-on methods has meant long hours and great amounts of physical work for Katherine. For someone who earned her bachelor's degree in 1947, she has maintained a healthy and active life and her active work contributes to her fitness daily. Katherine sits cross-legged on the floor to communicate directly with her students, she is always gathering interesting new articles and tidbits of information that will inform the ABC community, she is a model of excellent eating habits and a great vegetable lover, and she doesn't hesitate to help a child forge ahead with a project or a dream.

Cultivate life with joy, effortlessly.

51

Care for others without being
possessive

Wise teachers care greatly for their students, but they recognize clearly that these children do not belong to them. Parents, even those who may not seem to be in control of their children, are to be respected and given support. Their love for their children is not to be forgotten. In getting close to students, teachers do not attempt to compete with or downgrade mothers and fathers. Some teachers mistakenly think that they must not get close to their students, that their private lives must remain a mystery, and that the walls of the school demarcate boundaries of recognition. In the Tao, teachers recognize that their modeling does not end when they walk or drive away from the school.

Do not hesitate to get close to your students; allow them to know the various dimensions of your own humanity, but always show honor to the relationship of parents to their children. Maintain open access for parents to talk with you, to visit your classroom and communicate honestly about the progress of their sons and daughters. Parents who feel welcome also feel supportive of teachers, schools, and their children.

Joe goes out of his way to communicate with parents. At the beginning of every semester Joe sends a communication home with every student. It not only contains his policy about grading (as is required by the district), it also explains his philosophy of teaching, different methodologies and activities he uses, ideas about learning, and he includes phone numbers where he can be reached, when he can be reached, and a promise to return a phone call within twenty-four hours of receiving it. On back-to-school nights and during open house he arrives early and stays late to meet with parents. Occasionally he will be asked to meet with parents in restaurants, coffee shops, or even in a local park to discuss a problem privately with some student or some family matter or something wrong at school. The parents come to know Joe well and can communicate with him on several levels. One dad teased him, offering to buy him a Rush Limbaugh book to "straighten him out."

When one of his students, a baseball fan, arranged to go with him to a Thursday night Dodger game, another student, Charles, came along too; in his hand were two expensive tickets to a local charity's garden tour. "My parents sent these to you." On the other hand, another student, Alan, was very upset that his parents wanted him to stay home and get some sleep to prepare for a math test and his own game the next day. As a result Alan couldn't go to the game that he'd been planning to attend with Joe for a long time. He was very embarrassed, and spent the whole class period that day avoiding eye contact with Joe and acting unusual. When Joe asked him after class what was the matter and found out what the problem was, Joe told him he would have said the same thing to one of his own kids in the same situation. Joe is constantly reinforcing the work that parents do. Joe has two teenagers of his own, and his students always ask him what he would do in his own family's case. He tells them.

Act beneficially, without the intent to control.

52

*Enlightenment comes from valuing
what is small*

Wise teachers do not ignore tiny incidents or occasions. They learn how to handle them. From the child who comes to school with an untended scratch to the student who cannot leave his anger on the playground or the one who found a ladybug in the grass, all need to have your attention or a way to *feel* that they have your attention. Keeping the bandage box filled or providing a complaint system with cards that allows children to write about their problems can permit teachers to focus on other matters that may need attention at the moment. On the other hand, some things that may seem small provide "teachable moments" that can easily take priority.

Think about ways in which you can handle small things by giving responsibilities and outlets to your students. Recognize that many small things are important to children, while others can definitely "intrude" on your activities.

Maria is devoted to using class meetings of a sort that she learned at a workshop based on the work of Rudolf Dreikurs. She is convinced that the class meetings serve many purposes for her class: they promote oral language about topics that have authentic value for the students; they provide opportunities for the kids to do social problem-solving; they help build a sense of community for Room 27; and they model positive social behaviors for everyone. "If someone asked me to say what one thing has made the biggest difference in classroom management and promoting self-discipline, I'd have to tell that person about Class Meetings."

The agenda for any meeting is determined by a simple piece of notebook paper on a clipboard near Maria's desk. Any student who has experienced a problem that he or she has tried to solve through several measures but has not solved signs up: Name, date, brief description of the situation in three words or less. Students are allowed to sign up before or after recess times or before or after school. The class gets together to work out a solution.

The Tao is in the details.

53

Do not indulge in excess

Wise teachers know that problems have multiple causes and that the web of factors can be overwhelming to deal with. They do not, however, seek to deal with them all at once. They recognize that funds are seldom abundant and that reaching answers can only begin with one small step. Then they choose the step and take it. Surrounding inaction can allow the results of small actions to be seen and felt.

Do not choose elaborate plans when simple measures can resolve some conditions or point out what other steps are appropriate.

Joe likes to point out to his students that there really aren't many problems. There are just unsettled issues. Just to see something as a problem makes it seem as if there were trouble of some kind demanding a solution. If there are no problems there are no solutions. So instead of letting people think that there are problems, or that they have problems begging solutions, he leads them on a search for the part of an issue that is unsettled or the part of a story that is missing. Joe sometimes has difficulty with the image his psychology class has as a place where students can come dump their problems on everyone else. He knows he can't control the image, but he does frequently remind his students that if they stop seeing these things as problems and start seeing them as unresolved issues, they can feel more empowered to do something about them.

Schools themselves address many so-called adolescent problems: drugs, self-esteem, alcohol, gangs, family troubles, and social problems. The "solutions" often include assemblies, speakers, and workshops for teachers, parents, and students. Joe believes that it is helpful and important for individual students to share what the issue really is, what the workout is, and what possibilities exist for resolution. They learn that they can usually figure it out for themselves. They learn in Joe's class that they often don't need advice, they merely need support. Once they feel that support and gain some self-confidence, they learn that what they thought was a huge, unmanageable problem was really just a bump in the road. With a minor steering adjustment or a tune-up they can move on. "Take things one step at a time," Joe suggests. People can move through a difficult time of a relationship and work it out.

When a student brings up what at first appears to be a personal problem, Joe uses it as an opportunity to help the entire class walk through and work through whatever is in the way, one piece at a time. It's a stretch, Joe explains, but during the process he can allude to the historical method or the scientific method. He likes to point out that all they are doing in his psychology class is employing a paradigm for problem-solving that is used in even the most academic of disciplines. The students leave with a problem-solving model that they can apply throughout their lives. Joe knows that it is never a waste of time to deal with issues in the personal lives of his students. They can become grist for learning and teaching moments of the highest order. Often, in school, students are told to leave their so-called personal problems outside the classroom door. Joe sees these issues as inspiring opportunities for growth and learning.

THE TAO OF TEACHING

Joe always writes sayings on his chalkboard, little aphorisms for his students to think about. One that stays: "There is no solution; there is only the next question."

The complexity of a solution benefits no one.

54

One who is established in the Way
cannot be separated from it

When "born" teachers are recognized, their influence is great but not because their acts are powerful and overt. Not only do they remain dedicated educators, but their interest affects those around them in much the same way that rings surround small movements in still pools of water. Other family members frequently choose to become educators. The reputation of wise teachers becomes known in the community and their influence is shown in the ways that great men and women always dedicate their memories to educational experiences.

Do not think that, because your acts seem small, your influence is not great.

Katherine's class is known to parents far and wide. Her ways are known to children who go off in a multitude of directions, all of them grateful for having spent time in her primary classroom. They are police officers and teachers, executives and homemakers, college professors and vocalists. What they all have in common is a sense of self-esteem and efficacy that allows them to persevere in the face of difficult times.

A significant part of the environment in ABC is its set of highly involved parents. In arranging for frequent parent conferences at the start of the year and in setting up many types of workshops that involve the parents in learning about such things as art (with the district art mentor) to managing their children (with a volunteer MFC counselor), Katherine ensures that the parents become the best contributors they can be. After all, parents should be intimately involved with the education of their children.

The cultivation of the Way will extend beyond the classroom to family, community, country, and the world. What is well-established cannot be uprooted.

55

Stay in touch with your original nature

Wisdom allows teachers to examine situations in terms of external factors and intuitive reactions. "Having a feeling" about people and circumstances is not to be dismissed, but it can be weighed with a close examination of the conditions and measures that can be taken to deal with it. For example, when a student with a reputation for kicking other children is accused yet again of kicking an always-innocent child, the situation immediately suggests guilt. The kicker's claims of innocence could be easy to ignore in the face of apparent reality. In the Tao, the teacher develops and respects his or her intuition, and if feelings suggests taking a pause, the wise teacher will take the time to find out what really happened.

Get close to your students, for in doing so you can also develop intuition about them. It will guide you in situations where your instincts about your relationships will have power over mere circumstantial evidence.

Something that Maria treasures are her Friday friendly phone calls. She has discovered that when she talks to five parents (or guardians) a week, she learns about things that are going on with her kids, things that she would hardly know otherwise. Getting parents' perspectives and understanding more about the things that are affecting the children at home help her to speak and act wisely in class. Talking to the kids when they are at home (and when she is at home) helps dispel the notion that teachers live at school, and the chat broadens her perspective about the children's lives. Sometimes the TV is blaring in the background and the conversation is held in loud, almost yelling, tones, and it doesn't last very long. *"Yes, that's right, this is Richard's teacher! . . . Hi, Richard. You have been doing such a good job with your radio show. Thank you for working so hard. We all laughed a lot, didn't we? What was that? Oh, yeah. I'll see you Monday!"*

At other times the conversation is long—maybe too long, except that the parent needs someone to talk to, and Maria is placed in the role of "expert." She knows that it is usually better to listen than to give much advice, so she does her best to listen. "Yes, it must be hard. Uh-huh. I understand. Uh-huh. I hear you saying that you often feel like giving up. I'm sure you're doing your best. Sure. That's right. Well, the school psychologist is always glad to talk to parents. As a matter of fact, her number is on that sheet we sent home to all the parents today. Yeah. Absolutely. You can be sure of that. When he gets back from his dad's, tell him I called, okay? Good luck. 'Bye."

One student, Hoa, spoke no English when he came to Maria's class. He was a child who was full of anger. He would act very sullen in the room, his face taut and his eyes constantly cast aside. On the yard he got into fistfights. Hoa wanted to be part of the basketball games, but the other sixth graders wouldn't let him. One day, when he was turned away for the third time, he came inside and knocked chairs over as he walked to his desk. Maria went to console him, touched him lightly on his shoulder, but he pulled away and said nothing. All Maria knew was that he seemed to listen to her when she talked to him at a distance: *You are upset. They have not shared. Games are for playing. No games are closed.*

So Maria worked with him. She repeated her ideas to the class. She had the kids join in helping their new friend. "We played games. We played Bingo. We did Language Experience every day. We built sentences and stories." By December, Hoa was a regular fan of *National Geographic*. One day, he was in the classroom library during a choice time and he began to yell, *"Me, me, me!"* Hoa was pointing to the picture of people being lifted by helicopter to a ship. *"Me, me, me!"*

"You were on one of these boats?"

"Yes, yes! Mom, Dad, brother. Not my sister. Not my dog. They throw my dog over the side of the boat. In his cage. They made room for people." Everyone in the class was interested and excited. Hoa had never said anything so loud or so long before.

Hoa would always have his homework done. Not that things were perfect—when Hoa got enough words he often argued with the other kids, but many aspects of classroom life started to fall into place for him. "In Vietnam," he explained, "you lean over a bench and get struck if you do not have homework. Here I hug a tree with thorns." One day, Hoa couldn't walk very well. His knees were swollen from being forced to kneel on rice. It was time to talk to the parents and Maria was glad that their school had had a recent workshop on the cultural aspects of discipline; she knew how to report and help the situation appropriately.

Gradually, Hoa became "a truly valuable classmate." He was willing to help. He was a leader with other kids on the playground, very much like a regular referee. Hoa used a technique that he described as, "I separate them, I talk to them: 'What is the problem?' " Hoa used all the problem-solving techniques that students had been taught in class, and more. He would even help other teachers and supervisors, and he became the person to call upon when a problem erupted on the yard.

Another way that Maria finds very helpful to get to know her kids is to pay visits to their homes. She knows that it has made a difference in her success with students many, many times. She is clear about the two-way benefits. She always has another teacher —her aide, her principal, someone from the school—go with her, but she makes sure that her visits are not "problem" visits. She takes her class list and drives through the neighborhood. The kids run out of their apartments and stand in the yards of tiny frame homes and large stucco structures. *"¡La Maestra! ¡La Maestra!"* Teacher visiting the children's homes is a special event. As Maria explains, "All of the kids recognize you and run beside your car. They all beg, 'Come to my house.' Then I park and ask, 'Can you tell me where George lives?' 'He lives here behind this house. It used to be a garage.' If you arrive at one house, they follow from house to house. Everyone knows you are there." Inside, the TV is going full blast. A parade of children walks between mom and the visitors. Kids carry snacks and stare at the teacher.

One mother who had been a teacher in Mexico was very helpful in developing some math projects to do at home for the children. Another mother served homemade tortillas with cinnamon and sugar. At one home a chicken walked across the kitchen floor. One mother told Maria that *Maria* should tell her husband that she, the mother, should use birth control. She was pregnant again with their eighth baby. The teenage daughter was serving as a translator and because the mother didn't want the daughter to know exactly what she was requesting, she talked around the topic in general words. She said that she was pregnant and she did not want any more children.

The Clover Apartments, at the edge of the strawberry fields, were built after World War II as homes for defense workers. They were never meant to be permanent structures, and when it rained the area turned from its usual gray dust to mud. Irma's home consists of a small living room that holds a couch and a TV, a bedroom big enough for a bed only, and a bathroom at the end of the hall. Mom and Dad sleep on the bed, the oldest child sleeps on a mattress at the foot of the bed, and the rest of the children sleep on the floor in the living room. The Formica table in the kitchen area seats four, but since there are eight children, the sink is constantly full of dishes from one meal or another because the family eats in shifts.

At Gloria's house there is a swimming pool in the backyard. The two cars in the driveway are a Cadillac and a late-model Toyota. Gloria's dad has a flourishing business and Mom is committed to staying home. She invites her daughter's teachers over for lunch each semester as a sign of her appreciation. The home is full of mirrors and gilded picture frames. When Maria arrives the table in the sunny dining room is set with fine china. As Gloria's sixth-grade teacher, she joins six other people, one man and five women, on upholstered mahogany chairs. The food is Greek. Music pours from a large stereo system in a wall unit that runs the length of the living room.

Teach in multiple ways, in harmony with the diversity of your children.

56

It is impossible, with a person who has gained harmony, to be indifferent or intimate, to harm him or benefit him, to disgrace him or honor him

Wise teachers learn to be self-accepting and reflecting. Therefore the forces of political antagonism or favoritism have a neutral effect upon them. The relations of others are important, but their impact is seen in a different light. What might upset another person as being poor treatment or wonderful treatment is seen only as relationship. Wise teachers are oblivious to the feelings that might arise in others who are not in the Tao.

As you grow to be your own best judge, the judgments of others will mean less and less. Criticisms, even compliments, will not be taken personally and you will remain detached enough to maintain balance and evenhandedness with both fellow teachers and students, with your friends as well as your enemies.

At a teachers' meeting one morning, when Maria talked about how she liked hands-on experiences for math instruction, she realized that two of her colleagues were talking with each other in low voices. Not only were they rolling their eyes, but they took out homework papers and began correcting them with gusto. Maria talked about how she liked using Cuisenaire rods for learning multiplication and Geoboards for learning geometric shapes and measurements and she gave her colleagues the choice of which manipulable they would prefer to work with during that workshop session. In spite of the good experience that many of the teachers had, the same two colleagues left the meeting muttering, "What does that have to do with learning the facts? Are we telling the kids they don't have to memorize?"

Maria realized that she had not won their understanding. Her principal stopped by her room later to chat, briefly acknowledging that Maria's presentation had been very helpful. Since the children in Room 27 were engaged in their workshop work, the two educators talked and came to an understanding that Maria's role was to continue to pursue success for her children and that her administrator would converse with the two negative teachers and how manipulatives could work for them.

In the meantime, as the semester went by, Room 27 came to do *many* things with Cuisenaire rods, and the kids built 12" × 12" decimal Geoboards for the next class. The students devised problems for one another and they made a *Stump the Class* book for the class next door. Three parents said that they were glad to come and help supervise the hammering of 111 nails per pine board. And, in the long run, Room 27 came to have deep understandings of concepts that affected day-to-day life with mathematics.

Identify with the changing, natural world to achieve inner truth.

57

Succeed with encouragement, not prohibitions

Every restriction can be met with resistance. The Tao is not dependent upon rules for success; neither is it the way of non-action. Wise teachers do not post a dozen rules, even when they have been formed in consultation with the students. Rather, they develop the most important concepts—perhaps three—that can positively guide their class. Such things as, "We honor other people," or "We respect learning," have greater power than "Don't touch other students," or "Don't talk while you are working." Positive precepts can always be true.

When you post rules on your classroom wall—and that is a good idea—do not allow them to become a rambling list of *Don'ts*. Children are quick to test the exceptions and expect consequences to be applied uniformly to all offenders. Post rules and consequences that are developed jointly and that are positive. Positive rules motivate and generate positive behaviors; negative ones produce hostility and resistance.

For several years, Joe has had his students read and, if agreeable, sign a Statement of Responsibility that outlines specific rules of behavior to be followed during class. For example, "I will be in class on time." "I will turn in work when it is due." "I will partici- pate in class discussions." At the bottom of the statement are three blank lines where the student can write exceptions to any of the rules stated above. One girl had ice-skating lessons in the morning before school and could not make it in perfect time to first period, so she wrote that on her statement. Another student read the morning announcements over the school's PA system, so he would be late for the next period every day. This exception policy allows students with physical or educational handicaps, such as deafness, an opportunity to be a fully functioning member of the class despite personal difficulties. Joe's students also know that they will not be sent to the office, ever. They will not be assigned detention or kept after school or in any way ridiculed or denigrated in class, so they are assured that they will retain their integrity and their confidence. Joe pays attention to positive learn- ing experiences and outcomes, not to rule-making and enforce- ment. He figures that if the students are engaged they are not going to need many rules—just rules of engagement!

The more restrictions people have, the more outlaws will emerge.

58

A wise person governs in
non-discriminative ways

Discrimination implies that there is a preference for some or a prejudice toward others. Wise teachers examine how to provide classroom systems that treat students equally. In doing so they may find that equal treatment results from unequal interpretations of rules. The expectation for all children to stay in their seats and not wander around the room may be an unfair expectation for some. In getting to know students well, teachers can come to know what instructional contexts are tolerable, possible, and desirable for various individuals. In knowing themselves well, teachers know what alterations in their own preferred style of teaching will be necessary to accommodate different children.

Do not discriminate against some children by permitting rules to have singular interpretations. Only rules that involve safety require unilateral, unquestioned, uniform obedience.

Katherine and her longtime friend and aide, Marlene, have always brought singing into the ABC program. Some songs have become favorites year after year. Marlene has a file of poster-size word boards that she rests on a special large wooden song box to guide the children when she leads the singing several times a week. One song is a favorite with the children and the adults as well, and Katherine believes that this song is perhaps an appropriate theme song that expresses what ABC is all about.

Flowers Are Red

The little boy went to the first day of school
He got some crayons and started to draw
He put colors all over the paper
For colors was what he saw.

And the teacher said, "What you doin', young man?"
"I'm painting flowers," he said.
She said, "It's not the time for art, young man,
And anyway flowers are green and red.
There's a time for everything, young man
And a way it should be done
You've got to show concern for everyone else
For you're not the only one."

And she said,
"Flowers are red
Green leaves are green
There's no need to see flowers any other way
Than the way they always have been seen."

But the little boy said,
"There are so many colors in the rainbow
So many colors in the morning sun
So many colors in a flower and I see every one."

"Well," the teacher said, "you're sassy
There's ways that things should be
And you'll paint flowers the way they are
So repeat after me . . .

THE TAO OF TEACHING

"Flowers are red
Green leaves are green
There's no need to see flowers any other way
Than the way they always have been seen."

As the story goes on through two more verses, it becomes a sad tale of the boy who is considered sassy and gets put in the corner, and who in the end is broken by the system because of fear. In the end he can only paint flowers "in neat rows of red and green," and he says, "There's no need to see flowers any other way/Than the way they always have been seen."

Overbearing government makes for indifferent people.

59

Be frugal and accumulate virtue

The classroom that collects virtue keeps track of the good things that occur. Students are frequently tracked by the negative things they do, so much so that their virtues can be overlooked. Wise teachers encourage students to record, in their journals or on other records, the ways in which they show kindness to others, and select wise strategies for learning in a community of learners. Such teachers help students to look for, make note of, and report on acts of generosity and virtue found in the news in their neighborhoods, in town, or in other places in the school.

Help your students to see what a good place your classroom is. Collect anecdotes about acts and activities that demonstrate how you follow your positive classroom rules.

Joe believes that kids need to know about positive role models. He loves to use the newspaper, not just for the front-page news but for the many human-interest stories that can be found. When the Teacher of the Year for California was written up, the kids talked about her and the troubled youth she helped. When a local senior citizen, Joe's friend Eva, died, Joe had his students read her obituary and he put it on the wall. She had been active in local charities and ecology movements and had volunteered her time in count-less ways to individuals who needed attention. A local woman, Rosie, who runs an after-school school in her garage not far from their high school, was honored by the U.S. government for her efforts in helping immigrant children. The students are in the habit of looking for individuals who are great role models. One boy recently brought Joe an autographed book from Rosa Parks as a present.

Joe also has a wall of fame in his room. He put a piece of masking tape down the center of a bulletin board and on the left side go news articles about young people who have done out-standing things. Not just good deeds, but good deeds that make a difference. People nobody knows about. In 1988 a girl from Joe's high school was told she couldn't be on the varsity soccer team and also be a cheerleader. She went to the school board with her parents, arguing that she could keep up her 3.5 grade point aver-age as well as afford the time, and she got the policy changed. A young man from a local beach community led a successful youth clean-up campaign. A Vietnamese youth manages two furniture stores in a nearby city. Eagle Scouts do a number of local proj-ects. The idea is that one person *can* make a difference. Kids contribute ideas too, handing articles to Joe. Joe honors his own students in very subtle ways—with smiles, facial expressions, brief comments. Joe recommends that all of his students keep journals, but he does not collect them. They are not part of their grades.

Acquire good habits early, and they will serve you for a lifetime.

60

A wise person will not harm others

It is said that "Ruling a large country is like cooking a small fish." Similar carefulness must be shown in guiding a class full of diverse students. Heavy-handed treatment can destroy what is good and whole. Hurting others is not possible for wise teachers. They find ways to make the offensive acts of others seem inoffensive. The child who calls out during a lesson that there is only one minute until recess can be thanked for wanting an organized class. A suggestion for more appropriate ways to help with the organization can be given at another time in private.

Always try to see your relationships as you would see the liquid in the glass—half-full, not half-empty.

Maria knows that because her students are all so different, she deals with "difficult" students (and teachers) all the time. The intrusion of others on each other's time and space is fine until someone does something that is seen as rude, or as breaking the rules. Then there is a problem. Nevertheless, Maria tries not to see other people as wrong and herself as right. She attempts to see how *they* think they are right. Her "attitude adjustment" trick has helped her in many situations where people are doing things that would be perceived as very wrong by many people. Before she ever judges a person or situation, she thinks and/or listens first.

Juan worked for days on his Mother's Day project, coloring with chalks and glue until he had a beautiful flower composition on a black background. However, when it came time to send the pictures home, he folded his up into a packet small enough to put in his pocket. Maria remembers being horrified and she was about to lecture him on how thoughtless it was to ruin his mother's picture and spoil the efforts of his hours of work. She made herself listen instead, so she asked, "Juan, can you tell me why you folded up your drawing? I am worried that it will get spoiled."

Juan smiled at Maria and said simply, "This is going to be a secret. My mom doesn't know I made it and she won't see it when she looks in my backpack. I will put it under my bed and *really* surprise her on Mother's Day!"

Maria, who had been about to scold Juan for the folding episode, said, "I know she will appreciate your hard work," and walked away.

Another one of Maria's students is a girl, Barbara, who was constantly mistaken for a boy, and had been dressed in jeans, sneakers, and a sport shirt every day for as long as anyone could remember. Because Barbara's hair is trimmed short, and because she is a star athlete and she gestures with broad, masculine sweeps of the hand, everyone at the school calls Barbara "the Boy." In the classroom, Barbara makes a point of yelling out for attention. She even goes so far (when Billy says, "You wouldn't know what a dress looks like, would you, Barbara?") as to jump up and stand above Billy's desk, glaring down at him with arms crossed and face taut.

Maria, tired of her behavior, had several private talks with Barbara, and each time she received a "Sorry, it won't happen again." But it did. And at the same time, Barbara's journal entries, which had been full of sports scores, great games, and tales of cleaning and scrubbing for other people as part of her family's cleaning service, turned to vague descriptions of "what a wonderful teacher Maria is; no wonder her students love her. She is a beautiful teacher. People love her. She is lovely and kind. She is special. Her family must love her."

Then Barbara started to show up in front of Maria's house, miles away from Riverview School, once on a Saturday morning, a Sunday afternoon, another Saturday morning. Barbara arrived on her bicycle, rode up and down the street seven times and then parked in front of Maria's house and just sat there until someone noticed that there was a large, muscular girl sitting out in front of the house. Maria asked her if she wanted to help pick some weeds on the hillside since that was where she was headed. Then, in between the long pauses in conversation that were filled with the tiny noises of roots being pulled from the dirt, Barbara pulled tiny bits of information out of her memory and told Maria that things were pretty bad at home. She was always tired. Yes, they worked long hours each evening. But something else was wrong. Something bad was going on. Barbara's sisters were sad. Barbara wasn't going to let it happen to her. She was just like a boy, after all.

Maria reported the potential sexual-abuse situation. And the family, after long years of silent suffering, changed many things when Barbara's father was sentenced.

Do not spend all your time weeding.

61

In placing yourself low, you take over others

Honoring one's students and showing pleasure in their company are wise practices. It is part of the Tao to develop the "feminine" attitude of being still, willing to take a lower position. Such ways are also possible with colleagues. Sometimes it means finding ways to get to know them that are unconventional—attending a piano recital or motocross race of a student, expressing a desire to visit another teacher's classroom. There is much to be learned from entering into the contexts of others' worlds.

Do not hesitate to express your interest in getting to know others or to admit that you have much to learn from them.

Katherine gets to know her kids and her families very well. The process starts long before the child's first day in ABC, for kids and parents visit the class weeks or months earlier and spend time making sure that this is the place for them. No child starts without a long parent-teacher conference taking place first. Katherine has a sense of each child before he or she starts, understanding not just things about the child's strengths and needs, but also knowing what family forces might be in effect. Is this a two-career household? Are there other brothers and sisters? What health needs are there?

Katherine always accepts challenging children for ABC. Even though there is extra work involved or a need to problem-solve with parents on a regular basis, she is game. When a child with muscular dystrophy entered ABC, everyone worked to accept her, to accommodate her special needs for bathroom and seating, and to treat her like everyone else when, at most times, that was just the thing to do.

Be tranquil to receive all that will flow your way.

62

The Tao never rejects a bad person

Wise teachers learn that there is no bad person, only one who has made poor decisions. They help students to see what alternative decisions might have been made. They learn what good decisions have already affected the lives of others.

Accentuate the positive. Help eliminate the negative. All students are worth your effort. Some need affection and kindness when they seem to deserve it least.

Eddie is someone else who creates tension wherever he goes. If five kids are out after the bell, one will probably be Eddie. At breaks, campus supervisors will keep their eyes on him alone. He is "nailed" immediately if he comes to school with baggy pants, even though other kids do so without comment from any authority. But the supervisors manage to criticize only him, not the other students. A former gang member, he is now paying $3,900 to get his tattoos removed. He is the student who always has more to say. He is very confrontational. He is also one of the brightest students. He is the most aware. One brother is in jail, one brother is dead, shot to death last May. Eddie himself has been shot and he walks around with three bullet holes, one in his back. Shortly after he moved to Joe's high school from L.A., twenty of his former gang members showed up on campus at lunch to intimidate him. He started to walk across the campus, then he turned around and headed back to his new friends on campus. He shared in class later that day that turning away from his "home boys" was a breakthrough for him. They haven't been back since.

Eddie barely gets to class on time, and one day Joe called his home about an absence. Joe got his dad—a man who says he wants his son to be put in jail—on the phone. His dad was yelling at Eddie. "Dad, I was there!" Eddie said, and his dad shouted several times to his son, "Shut your fucking mouth." As it turned out, Eddie *had* been in class. A student aide had mistakenly marked him absent.

He responds positively all the time. He is always with Joe. He frequently exclaims out loud, things like, "God, I never knew that! That's great!" The kids say, "Wow, is he smart." After school Joe says to him in private that he doesn't have to respond to *every-thing*. Although Eddie talks out in class a lot, he seldom writes. He says that he can't, so one day Joe sat down with him and asked, "Who would you like to say something to?" "I want to talk to my brother in jail." As Joe tells it, he wrote a letter to his brother that was incredible, poignant, with interesting sentence structure, proper usage, and he mailed it to his brother right after school. Joe has kids share their writings in class often, but Eddie didn't want to share his letter.

Eddie argues a lot in class and talks about his home boys. "I don't talk to them now." He uses the word *fuck* a lot of the time. His voice changes in rhythm and tone, "Hey, man, what's happening, fucking this, and fucking that." And someone will respond, "I was in this town before you." "You never seen nothing. You don't have three bullets in you." When these outbursts occur, Joe waits a bit and then says, "Eddie, that's enough." Joe, an avid fisherman, explains that when you hook a big fish in the ocean you let it run a little bit. And it is critical to know when to set the hook.

Eddie is in so much turmoil. Early in the semester, Joe told him that he might want to keep a journal. He just suggested it. Eddie got a journal. He keeps it with his books and he brings it to class, but he keeps it out of sight. He wants out of that other life. He buys his own clothes now, shirts with collars. Most of the home boys drop out of school, but Eddie is going to graduate. He also is going to a prom for the first time. Where he lived before, it would have been too dangerous, with guns and drinking. So two short-term goals for Eddie, graduation and prom, are being fulfilled.

He walks past Joe every day, shakes his hand. "I made it today. Hey, Mr. Adams, see you Monday." He always says *Mister*.

A wise person abandons no one.

63

Repay hatred with virtue,
deal with the big while it is still
small

In the face of a hostile student a wise teacher speaks only kindly, yet with clarity. Saying positive things to a child that he or she might not wish to dispute, such as, "Your anger is unusual. Something unusual has happened," or "You are usually a thoughtful person. You must have been upset to change so," or "You have talent in diplomacy. I want you to use it" can help to defuse situations. Before problems escalate, they must be attended to, or an appointment for discussion must be made. With few schools able to hire many counselors, students must have other adults with whom to relate and examine their options. Small problems that fester or that have the attention of parents only in their perspective outside the school context can become unnecessarily large.

Set aside a time each day during which you are willing to listen to students' problems. Students can also help with suggestions, advice, and comfort for one another. Expect the unexpected and you will not be surprised by what happens each day.

"How do I feel today?" Katherine asks everyone, and children raise hands to share thoughts and possibilities. The children, who have been trained very clearly and carefully to use "inside" voices and to use their time wisely to complete their work, can gauge how Katherine feels, even though her expression is carefully composed not to give away her thoughts. "Sad," several reply. "We were too loud this morning." Or noticing the sheets of partially drawn-on papers in her hand, they reply, "Sad, someone has been wasting paper." Or, on yet another day: "Happy. Everyone was working well getting a lot done this morning." Katherine is dedicated to the proposition that group time is the right time to share emotions and she is convinced that children can learn to deal with their feelings better if they are able to communicate about them and talk about how to cope with them. After the children have spoken Katherine goes on to detail just how she does feel, and she may take the next five minutes to explain exactly why her feelings have developed and what she believes would help solve the upset or else she details how pleased she is with the situation.

This sharing of emotions permeates the very important activity of sharing children's writings from their writing books. Katherine may read a passage from a child's work done the day before. Going over children's writing carefully with Kim and Marlene is a daily process that takes up a great deal of after-school planning time and is also ongoing throughout the day as children work on their various pieces. The content of the children's work is very important to the adults. Although editing for correctness is part of the daily look at each child's writings, the adults' conversations about the work relate to children's ideas. At carpet time, Katherine reads a few passages that she has selected. She calls up each individual writer to stand by her side, embraced around the waist by her arm as she asks him or her to respond to open-ended questions about his or her work.

Cara was hurt when her good friend did not ask her to spend the morning in the blockhouse with her and two others. Katherine works through Cara's feelings, and whereas some classrooms handle personal hurts and affronts as outside the curriculum—and sometimes never handle them at all—Katherine believes that dealing with personal problems should be an important part of the classroom business. With the child's permission, the hurt is made public, and the children involved, as well as others in the class, are asked to suggest how the situation can be helped. Eventually, an agreement is made to have Cara tour the blockhouse. And later, she does.

When Deron is upset that a boy came by and hit him in the arm for no reason at all, he handles his anger by writing about the situation in his writing book, and Katherine not only commends his handling of the situation, but she speaks of the growth in Deron from last year. She recalls how he would have been angry and difficult only a short year ago, and the children who were around to remember nod their heads in agreement. Deron, an Oldest, is growing in emotional strength and it is no secret that things didn't go very well last year. Katherine often refers to shared events of the past. That ABC has an ongoing culture is always evident, and children new to the class get to know events and people from the past through Katherine's frequent recollections.

Aside from the individual choices children make to work with one adult or child and whole-class times on the carpet, there is only one other social arrangement that occurs for ABC children. On most days, the class is divided up for a short time in the afternoon. Oldests and Olders go with Katherine to the east end of the room to listen to the next installment of a chapter book or to a series of stories. The Youngers and Youngests go to sit at the west end of the room to listen as Kim reads stories that are more in line with their ages.

In the event of discord, deal with the big while it is still small.

64

*Put things in order
before disorder arises*

Wise teachers help students to institute routines and organize their work materials. They remember that "a journey of a thousand miles starts with one step." Keeping a tidy classroom on a regular basis means that the environment is pleasant, and that proceeding through many different projects becomes possible. In the Tao, materials are ready and methods for students to obtain them are easy and depend little upon the effort of the teacher. The best systems will depend upon non-action of the teacher, for student enterprise will be more effective and personal.

Be prepared. Attend to tasks before they grow to dimensions that are difficult to handle.

Maria is not a fastidious housecleaner, although she knows some people who are. She even makes jokes about how she "never gets far enough to alphabetize her shoes or wax her garden hose . . . or keep up with the laundry." Still, she is someone who knows the importance of an organized classroom, and she finds that it is a healthy practice to keep things relatively dust-free. Her procedure over the years is to make sure that every child in the classroom has a job that provides a definite service to the classroom community, both for preparing and executing activities as well as for cleaning up. She has always befriended the school custodians so that they understand and support her program of student involvement, and so that she can understand what their constraints are in working in her classroom.

One job that she can't do without is that of the classroom secretary, a student who reminds both Maria and the class to do things and someone who helps Maria to organize sign-up sheets and materials. Maria never puts private papers or grade sheets in places where students might pry, but she does have photocopied class lists available for checking in homework or the trip money or the lunch count, and she has her kids do the major part of the work.

The jobs change from quarter to quarter, but Maria believes that each student needs to have a responsibility for a long enough time to do it thoroughly. Each person is given permission to alter the written job description once he or she gets a new position, but once that agreement is made, the job must be done as frequently as the agreement states. All of the jobs have variable days, depending on the class schedule of activities. On days with messy projects, the trash control person must work overtime. When there are visitors to the school, the sergeant-at-arms must be a host/hostess in addition to other duties. The pet caretakers are in charge of seeing who takes the rabbit and the snake home for the weekend; the snails, the fish, the frogs, and the mealworm colony can stay. The class librarians see that books borrowed from the public library don't get mixed up with the permanent collection. Every job has daily chores to accomplish. Every student's name is posted on the wall with his or her respective responsibility written.

Be cautious at the beginning and at the end of a new project. See things to completion.

65

*Do not try to rule
through cleverness*

Too much academic learning is not part of the Tao. There must be a balance between acquiring new cognitive concepts and doing other things that whole people do. A wise teacher provides time for the arts and for physical education. They are not seen as frills, for they are as important as scholarly learning in school. Not only is it healthy for each individual student to encounter a variety of opportunities, but it is also vital that each child has an opportunity to work in an area of strength. The eager runners, the colorful painters, the old man in the play, the checkers players, the dancers, and the soulful singers should have avenues for expression in school contexts.

Allow your students to experience wide opportunities. Do not withhold some activities as punishment.

Maria has the children help to set up "consequences" in her classroom. She explains that there are three steps to avoid consequences, which the children handle themselves. One step is that the kids help her to design ways to avoid trouble in the first place.

The class studies conflict-management techniques together, and some of the students have become experts at lunchtime meetings for students who want to serve the school as conflict managers. Another step is that the kids are involved in setting up classroom standards together. The fall is when there are several days of negotiating what the very best set of classroom rules would be: not too long, not too negative, not too babyish. Rules are not only posted, but they become part of the "Room 27 Handbook," a book of procedures and information that the kids help put together about everything from how to write a school heading to how to call a homework buddy to how to write a bibliography entry. The third step is their system of class meetings that includes lessons about the actual design and administration of logical consequences for kids. The consequences themselves are suggested and approved by the students as well.

A true benefactor enlightens the people.

66

Do not be competitive;
do not oppress

This idea appears again and again in the Tao. Its message is clear, but it also has different flavors for interpretation. Wise teachers do not compete against one another for political favors; they work together.

If you don't compete, no one can compete with you.

Katherine says that she has been examining competition in her classroom. A turning point was when a workshop leader came to her school and taught how teachers can make most games non-competitive. "Let's see if we can get to one thousand points together. Can we all get the parachute to keep the ball in play? Can we get the ball to stay off the ground for another twenty throws this time?" Even in the spirit of cooperation the game is still fun, and everyone gets exercise. The idea of working together for the common good goes right along with Katherine's efforts to make ABC a supportive classroom community. She sees many ways in which the individual *and* the group must both be honored in order to promote citizenship. To her way of thinking, an individual may be respected without having to see him or her as a "winner." For that reason, she promotes daily activities that allow all of the children to have autonomy at some points, cooperation at others.

At the end of the school year she always allows the students to hold a talent show just for the children in the class and any interested parents who want to come. Everyone is welcome to perform and no auditions are necessary, but there are time limits. Every student may have three minutes on stage. Double acts may use as much as five minutes, but they are all subject to editing during rehearsal. The kids spend the last week of school practicing and enjoying one another's reading and acting, singing and dancing, joke-telling and puppetry, storytelling and piano-playing, ventriloquism and lip synching, and musical instruments, magic, and comedy. Katherine believes school should be in session until they all officially get out of school. She is not a teacher who puts everything away two weeks before school is out, and she figures that any teacher who allows learning to stop deserves the behaviors that tend to occur in some classes during June.

When the children perform for one another it is not to see who is best, but rather it is an opportunity to appreciate classmates in a different light. No one knew that Monica, usually a reserved Elder, could imitate a rock-and-roll singer so well, with a strong voice and a flamboyant wig. None of the adults knew before the talent show that Peter could play all sorts of songs on his cheeks by holding his mouth in different positions and striking his taut cheeks with his index fingers. And although everyone knew that Chris could tap-dance, no one had ever seen her do her whole act in costume before. It was a good way to end the year with a memorable set of days.

Emphasize unity and cooperation.

67

Have compassion,
practice frugality,
be willing to follow

Wise teachers risk caring for others. They acknowledge that acceptance of simplicity is a rich treasure. They are not interested in being leaders at all times.

Share your love with your students and your colleagues. Disencumber yourself from tastes that only create problems. Let others —students and adults—share leadership with you.

When Maria realized that she had seven or eight parents in her room who were new English-speakers, she encouraged all her parents to come in to help, sending messages home: "I'm going to be your child's teacher. Back-to-School Night is coming on September 14. Please come." Someone was needed to translate the notes into Spanish, so Maria asked the kids.

When Maria asked the parents to help her in the classroom, four parents accept the challenge: one mom from Mexico, one from Romania, one from Korea, and one from China. They spent the morning, many days a week, doing tasks to prepare materials.

Some of the jobs were rote, but they were things the students could not usually do: correct papers, run off dittos. The parents learned to play games with the children that didn't depend on language, like the place-value game Chip Trading. They helped to get art supplies ready and they helped children at the painting center. All of the mothers could understand more than they could speak, so they could listen to the children's questions and requests with some success. During Language Arts time, the parents would come to the various group sessions for oral language, reading, or writing. Maria included them in the groups as participants on an "even" level. When Maria offered an idea, she saw it as an opportunity for the children and the parent to say something too, if they wanted.

Maria was the first teacher in the upper grades to have parents work in her room. Other teachers were not so eager. "Why would you want parents around? They are more trouble than they're worth. They just want to compare their kid to the others. They want to snoop." But Maria loved having parents in the classroom. She could give the students more attention. The kids *loved* having their parents there. As she tells it, those kids had a "pride like a Pouder pigeon." Mrs. Chin came in and volunteered every day of the week, every morning, in order to learn English.

Maria took the four parents out for lunch at the end of the semester. They went to a local restaurant and the moms had difficulty reading the menu, although they knew quite a few words. As Maria anguished, "How do you explain potpie?" it took forever to order.

Mrs. Chin then became an aide at Riverview and Maria began to teach her English at recess some days. On the telephone, Mrs. Chin still can't be understood clearly, but she communicates well in person. Just recently she called Maria on the phone to say thank you for helping her to be a good speaker of English.

Share your leadership. Speak from behind so that you may remain in front without blocking the view.

68

*Your appearance or position does
not reveal your strength*

Just as an excellent warrior does not appear formidable nor does an excellent fighter become roused in anger, excellent leaders are humble. Wise teachers "steer the boat" by using the rudder in the back; they do not need to be at the prow to influence the direction being taken. Setting up a program according to students' wishes puts the teacher in a subordinate position, there to coach and support from behind.

Serve your students' needs in order to lead them. Be where they need you to be, at the right time and in the right place. Knowing this ahead of time takes some of the pressure off and teaching becomes easier.

Joe never stands at a lectern. He sits in a different place every day for Psychology. Even for AP Government he sits with the students at the same level in his swivel chair and promotes questioning. Joe will sit on a director's chair if his class size grows from this year's sixteen members to, as it looks now, well over thirty next year. Joe does not get angry at kids; he punishes them but doesn't single them out He does get frustrated at situations and he will say things like, "It bothers me when you don't listen," or "Please go sit somewhere else." But Joe always asks them afterwards if they understand why they were reprimanded. If they say they don't, he takes time to explain. It's important.

The students do not ask permission for bathroom privileges. They take one of three hall passes. One, in the shape of a shield, has been made by a student in wood shop. The others are blue laminated cards with Joe's name and room number. Joe is proud of the way in which the pencil sharpening goes on in the back of the room, with an electric pencil sharpener that doesn't make much noise. He does not collect homework personally. The box by the door is for dropping homework in. There is no out-loud complaining or exception-making. Communities are full of exceptions. There is a place for everything. Pencils in a coffee can are set out, already sharpened. Paper is set out. He does not penalize students for forgetting their own pencils and paper. He sees this system as a way to make it easier on himself; most students still bring their own things faithfully. As he tells it, you can put the food on the table but you don't have to put it on the plates for them.

The kids take responsibility for their room because they *are* the community. Yet the master is always there to assist them.

You do not need to be first.

69

Delight in non-confrontation

There is seldom a need to confront students directly and seldom a need to lose temper unless for effect. These are both choices that individuals make. Instead seek indirect ways to solve problems. Not only can students save face, but you avoid the lack of results often caused when hard feelings interfere.

When confrontation becomes mandatory, such as in a case where a student denies doing something that you have witnessed, express your regret at the conflict. Use positive goal statements. Instead of "You are lying," say "Always speak the truth."

When Stephen, a student of Maria's, first came from Romania, he would jump on his desk and on his chair. During recess Maria went to a group of kids from the room next door and got Hannah, a classmate of Stephen's who had come from the same homeland. Maria needed someone to translate and help Stephen get a good start. According to what Maria later found out, Hannah was very effective in the way she handled Stephen: "You'd better shape up. You are the shame of your nation. If you don't do things right, I'm going to kick your butt." And Stephen never walked on his desk again.

For herself, however, Maria has always admired the techniques advocated by Haim Ginott. After reading his books, full of parent-child and teacher-child vignettes and dialogues, Maria adapted his way of thinking to her own talking and relating to kids: "Pencils are for writing, not breaking. Please stop wasting pencils," and, "You are worried when your partner doesn't come to school. You wish that he would come and bring his part of the project." By taking a step back and understanding the feelings of her students, Maria is able to offer solutions to their problems.

A step back can lead to great things.

70

Be forthright and plain

Although the Tao is easy to understand, few are able to put it into practice. Wise teachers don't show off and they are no less wise for it. Doing things for the express purpose of getting attention or admiration from others can only create problems. Teachers who flaunt their personal wealth can predict with certainty that setting themselves apart will not endear them to others. However, using wealth for basic needs, such as special books, art supplies, tapes, and recordings, is in the Tao.

Keep your Rolls-Royce at home. Bring the hamster.

Although Katherine's class has received attention from television commentators and doctoral programs, she is very modest about what she accomplishes in ABC. She never accepts offers to be a guest speaker. She never promotes her program as something everyone else should do. She would never dream of putting on workshops. She is a teacher of children and that is what she aims to do well. If people want to visit, fine.

Katherine drives a 1966 Volkswagen "bug." It is a tan stick-shift, low-octane, *practical* car with great gas mileage and no lease payments. The license plate holder proclaims *Out of My Way*. She dresses in pants on most days because of the many hours she spends on the floor. She devotes her time and energies to her class and to her friends because that is who she is, a teacher.

Precious jewels may be found *within* the wise, not around their necks.

71

When you don't know, say so

Students respect the teacher who admits a lack of information at times. Wise teachers do not need to serve as the holders/transmitters of all knowledge great and small. Providing insights, provoking thinking and student questions, and supporting ways to obtain information are the essential tasks in the Tao. It is better to know (but think that one does not know) than not know (but think that one does).

You don't have to know everything. Just make sure that you do enough homework to know *something*. Your students will learn from what you do know. The rest, you and they can figure out together.

Maria knows a lot about a lot of things, but obviously she cannot have the answer to every question. She admits as much. On the other hand, it isn't a good idea to have too many "I don't knows." When a question is raised that Maria cannot answer, her advice is simple. She reminds her students that there is always a way to "find out." In this way the students come to feel not only responsible for the answers to difficult questions but accountable for the questions themselves.

The wise teacher shares in the pursuit of truth.

72

Be gentle to gain authority

Wise teachers give students long reins. They realize that under light pressure, growing gradually, students will be less likely to weary of the burden of learning new ideas. Opportunities to do nothing must be respected at times.

Be careful of the work burdens you place upon your students. Respect the frequent demands of busy lives outside of school. Do not assign hours and hours of homework. Coordinate with your colleagues in order not to create cumbersome, even impossible loads.

At a large-group sharing time of student writing, Katherine reads a piece that was written by an Oldest. It begins, "Miss H. is crazy. She reads the same story every year, *Crow Boy*. I told you she's crazy. I think every class should have a crazy teacher like mine. She doesn't give homework."

Katherine enjoys reading this spirited piece to the class and she capitalizes on its audacious message. "Boys and girls, if we don't have homework, does that mean that our children don't do work at home?" The children provide lively examples of how of course they do work at home, it just isn't called homework. Kids can always go visit different places or write special poems. They can draw pictures and read books, or they can bring in new pets. Students in ABC bring work from home often, in fact. There are no special restrictions or requirements; their lives away from school take on special meaning.

Respect your students and see what they will bring to you.

73

There is victory in non-competition

If every day is seen as an opportunity for growth there is no losing. Because plans are made with care, the day's activities can seem effortless. In the Tao, all children are aware of how the day will go, for they too will have opportunities to plan it.

Follow paths of least resistance. They can bring great reward.

Maria once heard someone admonish that it is "better to work smarter than harder." She decided that that was probably good advice, and she thinks about all of the ways she can cut down on her immense workload and still have a varied, interesting program for her students. She says that one of her guiding principles is simply to let the kids do the work. In following her instincts she has given up some perfectionism on her part, and of course she has given her students increasing responsibilities.

One area in which the students are tremendously helpful is in their set of classroom jobs. The kids are almost all conscientious about their selected housekeeping chores and dozens of daily record-keeping tasks that help keep books in order, kids' materials neat, and papers organized. The only drawback is that Maria has to watchdog so that some jobs don't interfere with academic work time. She has had to remind her librarians not to organize the lending cards when it is silent reading time. The erasers can go to the custodian's cleaning machine once a day, not twice. "The snake hasn't digested the last meal, for goodness' sake." Kids are kids, Maria tells herself over and over.

Another thing that Maria's students prepare each semester is their personalized lists of "Twenty-five Things You Can Do When Your Regular Work Is Done." She allows each person to custom design a list of important tasks and activities that he or she wants to do. The only constraints are that they need to be things that can be done in the classroom without bothering other people, and that Maria has to approve the list. From memorizing the capitals of the states to writing ten poems, from doing sit-ups to designing an electric car, from drawing a mountain scene in pastels to making a Popsicle-stick house, students have ongoing projects that they see as important.

The *Room 27 Weekly News* is also an activity in which the kids get to do the work. Maria is committed to sending a one-page newsletter home each and every week. Parents are always grateful for the communication, and Maria realized after some experimentation that when the kids did the articles, the paper got read more often and widely than if she typed the stories out neatly. Each week certain students have responsibility for writing brief descriptions, stories, and requests. The layout is predetermined. The kids write on 3" × 5" cards, or half-cards, in black ink. The cards are pasted on a sheet of typing paper with the regular masthead and logo (designed by Juan and Tamara), and Maria makes thirty-four photocopies on Friday mornings. Articles aren't particularly complex most weeks: "We need toilet paper rolls for art next week"; "Turn in all Outdoor Education money by April 12"; "Everyone liked Hoa's poem—here it is"; "The Star of the Week is Cory Watts. He was born in Downey, California. He moved when he was three years old. Cory's favorite sport is baseball and he likes to teach his dog Lady tricks. He also has a box turtle named Spike. Cory lives with his mom, Sarah, and two younger brothers. They go to Riverview too." Three or four times a year, though, the *Weekly News* becomes a "literary" work. Every student in Room 27 contributes a final draft of his or her favorite writing and, along with drawings, it all goes home to the reading audience of moms and dads.

Maria also has developed some procedures about how to incorporate her students' plans into each year as well as into each week and each day. She begins each year by inviting the children to describe the one or two things that they would really like to learn that year. Because her students are the "old" kids in the school, she has them write their responses as part of a simple "interest inventory" that she has designed. She also has devised a way to have the children help her to use the data wisely. After a full year Maria kept forgetting to gather lessons and materials that would address the goals listed in the inventories. She realized that the information was valuable and that she needed to get it out and organized right away. She began to have the students organize the data as part of their math lessons at the start of each year. The math teams rotate through the inventory center, and each group has a responsibility to use the inventories to collect and graph the numbers of students who are interested in various topics. For example, one group was responsible for doing the Reading Interest chart. Students who loved mystery stories were counted and entered, as were sports fans, horse fans, Judy Blume fans, scary story fans, and the kids who didn't like to read much at all. In addition Maria has the children help her calendar topics throughout the first semester (she doesn't like students to have to wait very long for their favorite to come up) so that she and the students can scout out resources. The most common way she uses the topics is to have each become the focus for a process called "Team Jobs," in which the entire class participates.

By following students' interests, instead of working against them, you will encourage their growth.

74

Obey your instincts

The laws of nature are powerful and are to be honored. Only when the ideas of leaders and natural authority conform can there be growth and success.

Use discretion in following directives. Question doing things that are harmful to the Tao. Decide ahead of time what consequences you are willing to endure for not following some orders. Then invest in those activities that foster real learning and which reap the most beneficial results.

Joe knows that there are institutional rules and understandings that are not always compatible with his philosophy and his approach. He also knows that there are times when he must get into the "right" way of being with students to encourage learning and personal growth. Constantly keeping in mind both the "rules of the game" and what is right for the individuals who are playing can be both frustrating and tiring. There are times when Joe will not compromise when it comes to violating his basic principles. He refuses to give Scantron, machine-scored tests, even though the guides that accompany the textbooks call for those. Relying on instinct as well as his experience that learning by its very nature is subjective and idiosyncratic, he would rather his students show they think for themselves than give the "right" answer.

In the end, all of his evaluations are personal. He interviews his students at the end of the grading period, negotiating with students with the understanding from the very beginning that the final grade will reflect both academic competence and classroom performance.

Joe insists on protecting the educational integrity of his classroom. He reminds people at his school that if interruptions are allowed and students are allowed to be summoned out of classrooms at the whim of an administrator, coach, or secretary, then the message to all students is that what goes on in the classroom is of secondary importance. On occasion Joe has been asked to release a student for a surprise drug test. He refuses to allow that. No campus supervisor is allowed in his room unless he or she can prove that there is an emergency that warrants a student's leaving. At first, his behavior raised eyebrows, but eventually administrative support acquiesced to respect his view.

Likewise Joe protects his own presence in the classroom. He does not comply with staff activities that pull him out of his teaching to pass out surveys or attend a staff meeting. Having substitute teachers is disruptive to the learning process, interrupts the natural flow of classroom activity, and sooner or later builds resentment in students. What goes on in his classroom in his absence matters. Joe is a teacher who will have over two years' sick leave accumulated when he retires.

You and your students will grow together.

75

Strive in moderation

Wise teachers avoid interfering with the lives of their students. They make suggestions with care and permit them to make their own choices. They learn to enjoy the children.

Your students will be easier to lead if you are relaxed and able to allow them their own decisions.

David, who is by far the most proficient reader and writer in first grade, spends immense amounts of time working side by side with Taylor, a boy who is at this point less proficient. The two of them are part of a set of five boys who are friends and who have a daily cooperative work relationship. When they write a story together there are agreements they have made to guide the process. Their rule is that the person who has drawn the picture is the boss. He dictates what the words of the story will be, but the writing is shared evenly among the boys. One boy does one line, the other the next, and so on. Since Taylor did the picture this time, he begins: "Me and David are . . ." Then he looks around and gets distracted.

David says, with some irritation, "Taylor, tell me what's next!"

When Taylor repeats the same words, David grumbles, "Yeah, I already wrote that!"

"Me and David are playing around on the vines," Taylor says. "Okay, David, D-A-V-I-D." David finishes filling one line and then it's line two. "Taylor, it's your turn."

"*Around.* How do you spell *around?*"

"You did it, pal."

"A-R-Oooooo-N—Na-na-na-na-na-na-na-na—Batman!—D," Taylor says.

"Finger space!"

"*On.* O-N. *The.* T-H-E. *Vines.* V-I-N-Z."

When it is time for a new line and a new sentence, the boys continue their reciprocal writing to complete, slowly, "Nat is on the hill."

Taylor ends, writing, "Period. By David."

David corrects Taylor: "That's too high. It's supposed to be down there."

Out comes the eraser and Taylor lowers the period to be in line with the bottoms of the printed letters.

David says he knows they're done because "That's all Taylor told me." This is clearly Taylor's story. David's stories that he writes on his own are all about different baseball heroes and teams or about Ninja Turtles. "When I help him, he's the boss. Then when he helps me, I'm the boss." David also explains that sometimes he writes with Bob, an Older, but that three boys aren't allowed to work together. One of the teachers will look over the story, writing in editorial marks at the end of lines that need fixing. Then the boys will use a marking pen to go over the words and "ink it in." All writing with pictures is inked in because of the reinforcement, and because it makes the writing visible when on display with dozens of other pieces hanging on walls and from ceiling wires.

In January David still writes his own stories about Ninja Turtles. By this point, however, his story focuses upon different details and it is literally six feet long. One hundred fifty battle-worn words later, the story ends: "Don said 'I hate it wene this happens.'"

Other children travel from setting to setting during the courses of their mornings, choosing to be near other children as they look at books and read on the couches or a beanbag (only two at a time) in the library. Working in pairs seems to work best. When three end up sitting on the couch to share one book, the process of eenie, meenie, miney, moe eliminates the third wheel. One day the eliminated child is Timmy. He is a flexible, friendly child, and he is a fan of *Where's Waldo* books, so he enjoys looking at one by himself in an easy chair after being excluded from the couch group. At other times, he will pore over them with someone else, often Dale, a Younger, but occasionally with an Older or with a good friend who is an Oldest.

After he does his writing Philip decides that he wants the usual arrangement for reading since it is a day his mom is volunteering in ABC. First she reads one book to him. It is one of the series of "value tales" about famous people by Spencer Johnson, a story of Louis Pasteur titled *Believing in Yourself.* Then he reads a book to her, *A Box Tied with Red Ribbon*, by Ruth James. It is a book that he has read before, but he likes it and wants to reread it. Philip really loves to read the words. Some others that he enjoys are Dr. Seuss' *And To Think That I Saw It On Mulberry Street* and *Come Over to My House*, by Theo Le Sieg. His mom comments that he has always been a patient listener, sitting still for a long time to hear lots of Dr. Seuss and chapter books, and that at home their conversations about books and reading have included pointing out the sounds letters make.

Value what exists by not striving for what does not exist.

76

Those who are flexible are superior

Rigidity invites resistance. There is strength in being able to bend. Things that are hard and brittle have death in them. Things that are supple and pliant are full of life. Wise teachers recognize the difference between having to back off and never having inviolate dictates in the first place.

Be gentle and supple in how you handle your students. Remember that all rules have exceptions, and often the exceptions contain the seeds of new learning.

Joe keeps his teaching flexible and open-ended. He is willing to bend and change what is going on at any time. He makes a point of being with his students, working among them. He is not separated from them by a desk, a podium, a table, or stacks of papers. In that way he can see and receive indications that something is not working and needs to be changed. Also, students are not afraid to speak up and suggest changes. When Joe runs into students in the hallways at school or at athletic and social events he asks them how they think class is going and what if any changes are necessary. Now and then he will meet with students at lunch or see them before or after school.

Jesse and Pat from the Advanced Placement Government class suggested one day after class that Joe not spend so much time on the details of each chapter. "Trust us, we'll read it. Just help us learn the basic concepts." In Philosophy, George speaks up and points out whether a reading has been too boring or vague. In one Psychology class Julia is the one. Joe calls her the "class mother" (as in scouting's den mother, sports' team mom, or elementary school's room mother). She provides criticism and suggestions, and with her as a model other students are willing to come forth honestly and comfortably. Part of every final exam, regardless of the course, is a class evaluation.

Former students also come by or phone to offer suggestions for Joe's classes in retrospect, based on realizations they come to have later in their lives. Recently Tray phoned from his California university, telling Joe not to change the type of open-ended essays he assigns in class. "They are exactly like the ones they give us here." Marie, who graduated from a private university and is about to begin law school, reminded Joe that his Socratic questioning gave her the self-confidence to do well in her senior class seminars at the university. Steve called from Washington to let Joe know that the sense of self-worth he picked up in his Psychology class has helped him become a top salesman at the auto dealership where he works. Joe hadn't heard from Steve in nine years.

When students call to suggest that perhaps he should do things differently Joe listens and responds with appreciation. He knows that, given some time for hindsight and reflection, people can offer suggestions that are valid and worth implementing.

The essence of life is soft and supple as a newborn child.

77

Excellence is its own reward

The Tao shares credit among all those who work together. Excellence is reward in itself. Bragging detracts from collective achievement.

Look for ways to stress equality. Never trade in self-praise or words that belittle others. In a learning community, there are no winners if even one member loses.

Joe has received his fair share of recognition, plaques, certificates of appreciation, and other awards. In almost every case he has brought at least one student with him to share in receiving acknowledgment. When Joe was asked to make a presentation at a state teachers' association Good Teaching conference at a university three hundred miles away, he brought two students along and they shared the platform equally with him. When he organized a Nuclear War Awareness week that involved several high schools, he insisted on having students photographed for several newspaper articles. After all, he insists, they did most of the work.

When the school asks teachers to nominate a Student of the Month, Joe prefers instead to choose an entire class for the honor since he feels that a student stands out only because the support and the activities of the whole group allow excellence to emerge in individuals.

The one who truly deserves credit claims no credit.

78

Be soft and weak, hard and strong

Wise teachers learn to shape themselves to their context. Unlike the teachers who try to be "one of the kids," they reveal certain aspects of their personalities in particular situations.

When in Rome, do as the Romans do—but maintain your individual identity.

Maria knows that it is important to be compassionate and understanding. She has learned that sometimes revealing her own softness or weakness can give her children permission to do the same. It is okay not to be perfect. She gives kids permission to be vulnerable. When she shares picture books like *Nana Upstairs, Nana Downstairs, I'll Always Love You, I'll Love You Forever,* she can't help crying in front of the children. They cry too. When they read longer novels together, like *Sounder* or *Bridge to Terabithia,* they share many moments of tension and sorrow.

Although she is a computer advocate and a devoted PC user, Maria is also known for making mistakes when it comes to things related to technology. As she tells the kids, "Machines don't like me." The kids always respond with appropriate directions or helpful hands. "You forgot to plug it into the cart." "It has to be rewound." "Just turn it the other way." "Try switching it to the other channel." Somehow Maria does indeed live up to her students' expectations, allowing them at the same time to be helpful in significant ways.

Maria tells about how one day Sheila was very upset after cutting her knee. The sixth-grader sniffed and snuffled long after the wound had been washed and medicated and bandaged. Maria had her sit at the teacher's desk on her rolling chair for a while. Sheila just sat while the class did a social studies project. The class went on, but she sat and sat. Maria explains, "There are times when you need to motivate kids to do things that they don't want to do because you know that it is the best for them. It isn't easy. You have to quiet them down. They need you to think the way they think and see the world the way they do. Do it in steps and don't expect it to happen at once, so be patient and go little by little. Expect to backtrack, but guide with a firm hand. Show lots of love. Explore the boundaries. Employ consistency with each child as an individual, but don't treat everyone the same. And whenever you say anything, follow though."

One must accept responsibility in order to lead. Guide with a firm but loving hand.

79

In attending to mistakes you may be missing an opportunity

Wise teachers hunt for successes. In reading their students' writing they always find the complimentable and agreeable. The mistakes can be found and corrected while working together with the students, or by students who are working together.

Use your red pen to write positive comments and suggestions—or use a green pen! Have students learn to be self-critical. Trust that they know when they've done a good job and when they haven't.

Maria makes her beliefs clear. She does not believe that anyone, including kids, responds well to criticism. She always tries to couch her suggestions for improvements into dialogues that contain plenty of positive ideas. She also refuses to belittle children in public. "When you yell at a kid, *you* are out of line. You must always apologize for being grumpy." Maria is proud she is not a yeller. Her kids are too.

Maria is convinced that modeling is a very important part of her work as a teacher. "We model in art. We model in math. We also read to kids, but do we model exactly what we want kids to do? If kids are going to read and write well, there has to be a lot done in the classroom. The children have to see *you* doing it." Maria also does not want to put any student into the embarrassing position of reading poorly. She does most of the reading when it is a large group setting. "I've had twenty years of practice," she tells the kids, and she reads with clear diction and dramatic variance. Not that students don't do a great deal of oral reading, but Maria prefers to have them work in pairs and small groups, where listening and reading are more intimate and easily negotiated. In Social Studies she absolutely won't let her kids read in round-robin style. "Does anyone else see how boring it is to have kid after kid mumble on about ideas that are truly exciting and deserve more?" Instead, she does have students tape-record various sections of the text. They read it through and practice first, and then she plays the tapes during class. Maria believes in the tape recorder as one of the finest technological teaching tools.

Maria also believes in the importance of journal writing, both for herself and her students. However, she has seen her students' journal entries from their past classes and she is disappointed in the short paragraphs and rapid handling of assigned topics. She is convinced that students' writing abilities will grow more from journaling if they write longer passages. Instead of using the school's small, standard-issue composition books, she has her students write in larger, bound notebooks that she bought for very little money at a local discount house. She explains that she thinks the attractive pictures on the covers and the large pages encourage more writing from her students. She also collects ten student journals a day in order to write responses to her children's ideas. She has tried other collection systems over the years but she found that responding to all journals each day was too much for her to keep up with, and collecting them once a week was too little reinforcement. Her comments to her students are designed to encourage them, so she tries to say specific words of a complimentary nature and she includes her own ideas beyond mere cheerleading remarks like "Yes! Wow! Great! Definitely!"

Maria knows that she is good with problem kids. Being an "NF" in temperament, she is the sort of person who sees potential in everyone. When Tamara arrived as a new student in Room 27, her mother told Maria that she was going nuts. The mystery of reading had escaped Tamara to the point that she was now belligerent about reading. As Maria soon discovered, Tamara's body language was stiff, her face was drawn shut, and she refused to read with Maria when she called her to come to a typical one-on-one conference time. Tamara had a million other things to do, and she simply ignored Maria. Maria let it pass for the time being. Maria saw that Tamara's former teacher had said that she was "slow," but Tamara did a pen and crayon picture the first day in class. It had shading. It had colors. "She is sharp. This is no dummy here," Maria thought.

After recess Tamara complained bitterly, "Those boys wouldn't let me play." After that the small, agile girl would walk out the door at recess and beat up anyone who didn't do what she said. She could walk up to any game of kickball and an argument would arise. Tamara would hit the other kids, or kick them. She would call them stupid and dummy. The kids in Room 27 got fed up, and by the end of Tamara's second day four of them had put problems with Tamara on the class-meeting agenda sheet. Maria did something she rarely did, and that was to consult with the kids and postpone the agenda items. She knew that Tamara had to get comfortable in her new setting before the class meeting would be effective.

Goodness is in harmony with kindness.

80

Be content and find delight in your home

Wise teachers make their own classrooms desirable places to be. They realize that children in other classrooms or from other years of their experience are not necessarily better, they are simply different.

Remember that the grass is not always greener on the other side of the fence—or on the other side of the school district.

Katherine enlists parents and students to prepare the classroom the week before school starts. It takes many individuals to carry in the huge potted plants that dot the room, the many animals that have summered in students' homes.

Sharing good literature is an important focus for large-group time in ABC. Katherine doesn't just read a story and talk about its actions and characters. How the story relates to the lives of the children is emphasized over and over. "Could this really happen?" Children's books are not just for children; their messages are valuable across the boundaries of time and age. When Katherine reads aloud, she bends the cover way back so that as she reads a page children can get a sustained look at the previous page. One bookcase is full of books that have been donated to ABC in the name of Allison, a former student's baby sister who was killed by a hit-and-run driver, and many of the books in this case have important themes touching on topics that can give the children insight into their own feelings and about the lives of people different from them. The bookcase is known as Allison's Bookcase and it is just one source of the many books that Katherine reads to the children. There is always one book shared with the total group each day, sometimes two or more, and these are in addition to the books shared at the half-class time. At the time of the death of Dr. Seuss, Katherine read a consecutive series of his books and reminded everyone of books shared in the past. She talked about the impact that his book *Oh, the Places You'll Go!* had had upon a former student who was about to go off to college. Books can make scary things seem less so, even for older people. Children may bring books in and Katherine follows through by sharing them, usually sometime during the same day.

Make your classroom a comfortable place, one in which good learning can take place.

81

True words are not fancy;
fancy words are not true

In the Tao it is recognized that truth does not have to be expressed in complex words. High-level deeds and philosophies can be expressed in the most basic terms. Similarly, helping other individuals can be accomplished through the most simplistic actions, from sharing food to sharing thoughts. Depth in learning is preferable to widely scattered bits of knowledge.

Teach your students the joys of helping others. Sharing new learning with others is one way to deepen understanding.

When Maria got to know her student Albert, she learned how ten people living in a two-bedroom apartment may have problems. Albert's cousins lived with him. Maria understood that they were not kind cousins, for they insisted on calling him names and generally made his life miserable. She felt sorry for him. His appearance was sloppy and he wrote English like a young child, every sentence full of misspelled and invented words.

She soon learned that Albert loved to draw. She gave him permission to draw in his journal as long as he wrote five sentences about what he drew by the next day. She used his drawings to illustrate notices that went home, and she invited him to submit a weekly drawing for a newsletter. "I need a drawing of plastic strawberry baskets to let the parents know that's what we are saving for our construction project this month." She had him add simple cartoon drawings to messages on the chalkboard.

In the meantime she praised him for his in-class behavior, for doing things on his own, for accomplishing work if all his sections were done. She explained how he could get an A+, and one day he did. It was the first A he had ever gotten in school. The assignment was always designed to fit his needs, and Maria would encourage him: "Just add two more sentences to complete your thought." But she made it clear that it had to be done.

Maria and her students visit the local convalescent home each month. The children of Room 27 walk a mile to spend an afternoon. Usually they leave after lunch and they return an hour after school lets out. The schedule was worked out as being the best for completing activities and for getting to do things with and for the residents of Hillcrest Manor. When Room 27 gets there, they go to the dayroom. As soon as all of the residents have come in, or have been pushed in on wheelchairs and rolling beds, the kids put on a brief play or sing a song or share something that they have been doing in school. Each student who wants to get to know an individual senior citizen has an opportunity to visit with him or her individually and bring something special, but all of the kids bring pictures and writings that they leave for a display in the hallway where the residents wheel or walk by. The plays they give are not always complex, but they are honest. The words and stories and poems are not always sophisticated, but they come from the heart. Here the circle of education is realized; the old learn from the young who learn from the old. Unity is maintained.

Fulfillment comes from helping others.

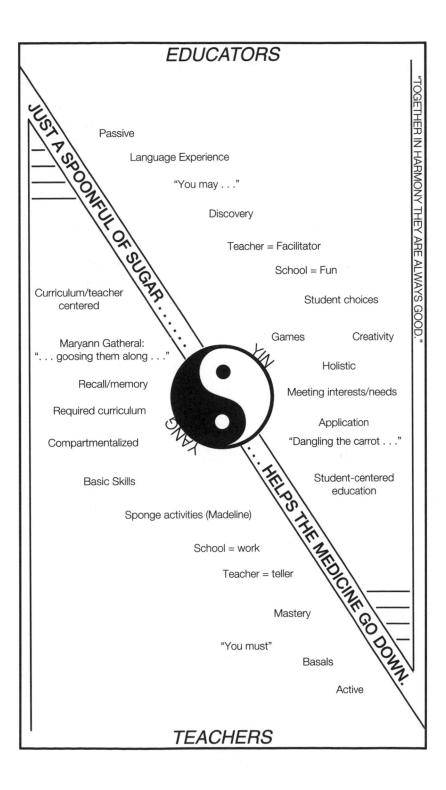

BIBLIOGRAPHY

Barnes, B. J. (1978). *Accountability: Taking account of human value.* Fullerton, CA: Institute for Early Childhood Education, California State University.

Biofeld, John (1978). *Taoism: The road to immortality.* Boulder: Shambhala Publications.

Chan, Wing-tsit (1963). The Lao Tzu (Tao Te Ching). In Chan, Wing-tsit, *A Source Book in Chinese Philosophy.* Princeton, NJ: Princeton University Press.

Cheng, Man-jan (1981). *Lao-Tzu: "My words are very easy to understand."* Richmond, CA: North Atlantic Books.

Costa, A. L. (1984). A reaction to Hunter's knowing, teaching, and supervising. In Hosford, P. L. (Ed.). (1984). *Using What We Know About Teaching.* Alexandria, VA: Association for Supervision and Curriculum Development.

Creel, Herrlee G. (1970). *What is Taoism? and other studies in Chinese Cultural History.* Chicago: The University of Chicago Press.

Lau, D. C. (1963). *Lao Tzu: Tao Te Ching.* Baltimore: Penguin Books.

Medhurst, C. S. (1905). *The Tao Teh King.* Chicago: Theosophical Book Concern.

233

BIBLIOGRAPHY

Pi, Wang (1979). *Commentary on the Lao Tzu*. Honolulu: The University Press of Hawaii.

Richert, E. Susanne (1986, February). Toward the Tao of giftedness. *Roeper Review, 8,* 197–204.

Watts, A., and Huang, A. C. (1978). *Tao: The watercourse way*. New York: Pantheon.

Wing, R. L. (1986). *The Tao of power*. New York: Doubleday.